THE NO-BULLSHIT GUIDE TO ETHICAL NON-MONOGAMY

For the Curious, the Cautious,
and the Currently in It

C.L. & D.J. AARON

COPYRIGHT

PUBLISHER'S NOTE

This book is intended for informational and educational purposes only and is not a substitute for professional legal, medical, or mental health advice. The authors are not licensed clinicians, therapists, or lawyers. Some topics discussed may be distressing. The case studies in this book are composites or fictionalized examples; any resemblance to actual persons is coincidental. To the fullest extent permissible by law, the authors and publisher disclaim all warranties and shall in no event be held liable for any loss or other damages.

CLAaron

First Edition: August 2025

Printed in the United States of America

10 9 8 7 6 5 4 3 2 1

ISBN 978-1-969182-00-6 (Paperback)

DEDICATION

For the inquisitive, the honest, and the kind.

And for those who give love without keeping score.

A NOTE TO READER

If someone gave you this book and your stomach dropped…

If you're here because your partner said, "I want to talk about opening up…"

Start with Chapter 4: This Wasn't My Idea.

That chapter was written for you.

This book speaks to many people—explorers, skeptics, and longtime practitioners. But if you didn't ask to be here, and your heart is in your throat, you deserve a different starting point.

Take a breath. Flip to Chapter 4. You're not alone. And you don't have to agree with anything to be respected in this conversation.

DISCLAIMER

This book is for informational and educational purposes only and is not a substitute for professional legal, medical, or mental health advice. The authors are not licensed clinicians, therapists, or lawyers. The guidance provided is a tool for reflection, not a prescription for your life. You are solely responsible for your own choices and their consequences. Laws regarding relationships, contracts, and parenting vary significantly by jurisdiction; consult a qualified local professional for expert assistance.

Content, Safety, and Responsibility

Some topics discussed, including consent, abuse, and grief, may be distressing. **If you or someone you know is in crisis, please contact the 988 Suicide & Crisis Lifeline (call or text 988 in the U.S. and Canada) or find global resources via the International Association for Suicide Prevention.** The case studies in this book are composites or fictionalized examples created to protect the privacy of all individuals; any resemblance to actual persons is coincidental.

Limitation of Liability

The authors and publisher have made every effort to ensure the accuracy of the information at the time of publication. However, we make no representation or warranties with respect to the accuracy, applicability, or completeness of the contents. To the fullest extent permissible by law, the authors and publisher disclaim all warranties and shall in no event be held liable for any loss or other damages.

TABLE OF CONTENTS

INTRODUCTION

NO ONE EVER TAUGHT US HOW TO DO THIS

We're handed a script for love–a story about finding "The One"–that often fits like something too tight and chafing in all the wrong places. We're taught the destination, but not how to navigate the messy, human journey. This holds true whether you're monogamous, non-monogamous, or still figuring it all out.

Whether you picked up this book out of curiosity, were handed it with a sense of caution, or are already living this life and seeking a better way, you are in the right place. This book is our offering to you, and to our younger selves–the guide we wish we'd had when we were starting out.

It's not a set of rules. It's a guide to thinking for yourself–to asking better questions, listening to your instincts without being ruled by them, and building relationships that are deeply, authentically yours.

This is a compass, not a map. The No-Bullshit promise of these pages is this: this work is complicated, and there are no easy, one-size-fits-all answers. This book is here to help you navigate the complex, often beautiful terrain of loving freely.

The No-Bullshit title is a contract. It's a promise between you and us:

- We will not sell you easy answers or utopian fantasies. Human hearts are messy, and anyone who tells you this is simple is selling something.

- We will not preach a self-sufficiency that ignores the power of partnership. This isn't a guide to needing no one—it's a guide to building connections sturdy enough to lean on.

- We will not waste your time on esoteric theory. This isn't a lecture on goddess energy; it's a toolkit for hard conversations.

- We will not trade the rulebook of monogamy for the dogma of the polyamory scene. This book provides the tools to design your own agreements, not a new set of rules to follow.

- And we will be honest about history. Non-monogamy is ancient, but Ethical Non-Monogamy—as a conscious practice—is new.

This is not a book of moral verdicts. You will see your own missteps in these pages—we all do. The goal is not to assign blame for the past, but to find a more skillful and compassionate way forward. This book is a tool for building, not a weapon to use against yourself or your partners.

This work begins with the assumption that we've all been taught bullshit, that we all believe some bullshit, and that we're all wrong about things. Many of the harmful patterns in these pages will feel familiar, not because people are intentionally cruel, but because we are all acting out unexamined scripts we inherited from our parents, our culture, and the media we grew up with.

The goal isn't to be perfect—it's to be honest, to be kind, and to be willing to learn. The true measure of a healthy relationship is not its absence of problems, but its capacity for repair.

This is not the path of least resistance. It requires emotional intelligence and self-awareness you may not yet possess. It asks you to be brave, to be honest, and to be kind—especially to yourself when you inevitably mess up.

This is the hard, worthwhile, and necessary work of building a life that is authentically, and ethically, yours.

The work starts now.

PART 1: THE FOUNDATION

CHAPTER 1: WHAT EVEN IS ETHICAL NON-MONOGAMY?

A NO-BULLSHIT DEFINITION FOR THE CURIOUS AND CONFUSED

You're here. You picked up a book with Ethical Non-Monogamy (ENM) in the title. Something in your life has shifted. It might not be a dramatic, earth-shattering event. It could be a quiet tremor in the dead of night, a question that surfaces in the space between sleep and waking: Is this all there is?

Maybe it's a tectonic plate that has already buckled under the foundation of your world, leaving you standing in the rubble of what you thought your life was. Or maybe it's just a tiny, persistent, hairline crack in the facade of what you were told love is supposed to be. But something, somewhere, broke the surface.

Maybe you're here because your partner of ten years, the one whose breathing next to you in the dark is as familiar as your own, said the words that changed everything.

Maybe it was a raw, fumbled, and overlapping series of thoughts that tumbled out, opening a door to a new and confusing world. A confession of deep, emotional entanglement:

> *"I think I'm in love with our friend, Sarah. I can't stop thinking about her. And I want to sleep with her. And I'm still in love with you, and I don't know what to do."*

Maybe it was a confession of a different kind of hunger, a desperate curiosity for sexual exploration:

> *"I love you. I love our life. But I feel like I'm dying inside. I've never been with anyone else. I want to know what it's like. I want us to go to a sex club, together. I just… want to feel something new."*

Or maybe, in their confusion, they reached for a script they'd heard somewhere else, a clumsy and devastating "truth bomb" that felt more like a verdict than a conversation:

> *"I love you, but I'm not in love with you anymore. Maybe I never was."*

Or perhaps you were the one who finally spoke those words, each one tasting like poison, relief, or a profound and terrifying confusion. In our stories, the villain is easy to spot. They are a caricature of evil, intent on our destruction. But in real life, the deepest wounds are often delivered by people we love, with tears in their eyes. The person speaking probably doesn't have a plan. They are grappling with feelings they were taught are impossible—that you can't love more than one person at a time. Because their feelings violate this core belief, their only conclusion is that their relationship must be broken beyond repair.

Their confession, however clumsy, is often not a verdict on the relationship. It is a terrified admission that *they* are lost. They are acting out the only script they were ever taught for this feeling: a monogamous one, which says that if you love more than one person, your primary relationship must be broken. Their plea, underneath the painful words, is often a desperate request to find a different map together.

Maybe you fell for someone you weren't "supposed to"—a friend whose laughter suddenly sounded like music, a stranger whose mind felt like a place you'd always known. The connection feels more vivid, more real than anything in years, and now you're living with a truth that's corroding you from the inside, a secret that makes your primary relationship feel like a well-decorated cage.

Maybe your partner cheated, and in the raw, gaping wound of that broken trust, you're now questioning everything. You're wondering if the betrayal was the act itself or the deception that surrounded it. That question is at the very heart of this work.

Or maybe you've just always felt like a bad fit, performing a version of love that never felt like your own.

Whatever your entry point, that experience has led you here. Welcome. This is where the work begins.

WHAT "ETHICAL" ACTUALLY MEANS

Before we go further, let's address a key piece of language. In academic circles and some communities, you will often hear the term Consensual Non-Monogamy (CNM). We use Ethical Non-Monogamy (ENM) in this book deliberately. The reason is simple: consent is the floor, not the ceiling. It is the absolute, non-negotiable minimum requirement for any interaction, but it does not automatically make that interaction ethical. You can consensually agree to a dynamic that is still fundamentally unkind, dishonest, or built to treat people as disposable. This book is not just about getting a "yes"; it is about building a practice of radical honesty, compassion, and care. That is the work of being ethical.

Let's get one thing straight. The "ethical" in Ethical Non-Monogamy isn't a simple switch you flip. It's not a certification you earn or a label you get to wear. It is the messy, ongoing, and often uncomfortable work of trying to treat people with fundamental decency and respect.

It boils down to one foundational ethos that is non-negotiable–**you must treat people as people**. That's it. That is the core of ethical practice. In the real world, this means seeing every person you interact with–partners, metamours (your partner's other partners), and casual partners–as a whole human being with their own history, needs, and capacity for pain. It means their well-being matters, and their consent is sacred.

In practice, this looks like:

- Not ghosting a casual partner after sex just because you're "not looking for anything serious."

- Using the correct pronouns for your partner's other partners, even when they're not in the room.

- Recognizing that violations like sexual assault are never acceptable, regardless of the context or relationship structure.

Non-monogamy is the *structure*—what you are doing. Being ethical is the *commitment*—how you do it: with honesty, compassion, and an unwavering respect for the humanity of everyone involved.

The goal isn't perfection. The goal is to feel everything—the joy, the heartbreak, the connection, the mess—and to navigate it all with as much honesty and grace as you can muster.

WHAT IT ISN'T: DEBUNKING THE MYTHS

Let's be clear, because the world is full of misconceptions.

- ENM is not cheating. Cheating is, by definition, a violation of an agreement through deception. ENM is the opposite: it is the practice of having multiple relationships based on a foundation of radical honesty and enthusiastic consent. If you're lying or hiding, you're not practicing ENM—you're just cheating with better branding.

- ENM is not a loophole for commitment-phobia. Wanting casual sex is valid. Not wanting a long-term partnership is valid. But calling something ENM doesn't make it ethical if you're breaking agreements or misleading people about your intentions.

- ENM is not a fix-it tool for a broken relationship. This is one of the most dangerous myths. Using ENM to salvage a deteriorating relationship is like trying to fix a sinking ship by drilling more holes in the hull. It magnifies what's already there—both the good and the bad.

• ENM is not a free pass for unchecked behavior. The foundational difference between any form of ENM—whether it's polyamory, swinging, or an open relationship—and what people call "promiscuity" or cheating is enthusiastic consent from all involved partners. Having multiple sexual partners is not the defining feature. The defining feature is that these connections happen within a framework of mutual honesty, negotiation, and respect for existing commitments. Without that ethical container, it's not ENM.

These myths often lead to another common misconception: that if ENM isn't cheating, it must be a free-for-all with no rules at all.

The Myth of No Rules

A common misconception is that this path is about having no rules. This couldn't be further from the truth. In many ways, practicing ENM requires more conscious agreements, boundaries, and understandings than a traditional relationship.

The difference is that you are no longer operating on the default, unspoken rulebook our culture provides. You are throwing that one out. But you are not replacing it with a void. You are replacing it with a framework *you* must build yourself, piece by piece, conversation by conversation. The work is not to become rule-free; it's to become a responsible author of your own rules.

A First Look at the Landscape

ENM isn't a single destination; it's a vast landscape with many different ways to live and love. This guide will tour the common styles you might encounter, such as polyamory, which focuses on multiple romantic relationships; swinging, which is typically centered on recreational sexual exploration as a couple; open relationships, a broad category of custom-built agreements; and solo polyamory/relationship anarchy, which prioritizes individual autonomy above all else. We'll touch on the basics of these here, but we will do a full deep dive into the specifics of each in Part 3.

NO-BULLSHIT TL;DR

- Whatever brought you here, your story is valid. The old scripts for love don't work for everyone.

- The "Ethical" in ENM is not a status you achieve; it's an ongoing commitment to treating people with honesty, compassion, and respect.

- ENM is not cheating, a loophole, or a fix for a broken relationship. The defining feature of ENM is the ethical container of consent and honesty that surrounds all connections.

- This isn't about having no rules. It's about the messy, worthwhile work of trading inherited rules for your own co-created agreements.

CHAPTER 2: THE MONOGAMY MINDSET

THE INVISIBLE SCRIPTS THAT SHAPE YOUR RELATIONSHIPS

So, you've decided to explore new ways of relating. You're curious, maybe a little nervous, but you're ready. You've intellectually accepted the premise of Ethical Non-Monogamy. And yet.

You're on a date with a wonderful new person, but you can't stop thinking about what your long-term partner is doing. Your partner has a fantastic night out with their other lover, and even though you said you were fine, you feel a cold, heavy stone in the pit of your stomach. You find yourself thinking:

"Why am I not enough? Am I losing some invisible competition I didn't even know I was in? I want them to be happy, but why do I also secretly want to be their favorite?"

It feels like cheating, even though everyone agreed to it.

Welcome to the **Monogamy Mindset**: the cultural conditioning running in the background of your mind, influencing your every move. It's the muscle memory you developed from a lifetime of exposure to a single way of loving. These automatic reactions of jealousy, envy, and insecurity are not a personal failing; they are evidence of deep cultural programming.

To move forward, we have to look back. We are about to drag the old rulebook we were all handed into the light, examine its foundations, and realize it's not the only one that exists.

THE TWO PILLARS OF THE OLD RULEBOOK

For most of us, monogamy wasn't presented as one of many options. It was presented as the only option. This isn't a critique of monogamy itself—a completely valid choice—but a critique of the unexamined, society-wide assumptions that box us in. You've been swimming in these waters your whole life; you only notice the water when you try to get out.

This "Old Rulebook" is built on two powerful, invisible pillars: **mononormativity** and **amatonormativity**.

Pillar #1: Mononormativity (The "One Partner" Mandate)

Mononormativity is the assumption that having only one romantic and sexual partner at a time is the only normal, healthy, or moral way to build a life.

16

It's tempting to think this is a timeless, biological truth about the human heart. It's not. The Western ideal of lifelong, state-sanctioned monogamy wasn't written to help you find your "soulmate." It was written to solve a very practical, and very unromantic, problem: who gets the farm when Dad dies?

As societies shifted to agricultural systems built on private property, it became critical for a man to ensure his land and wealth were passed down only to his legitimate biological heirs. Strict, enforceable monogamy for women became the answer. It wasn't a scripture about love; it was a script for protecting property.

Pillar #2: Amatonormativity (The "Romantic Supremacy" Mandate)

The second pillar has a fancy academic name, but the concept is simple: **amatonormativity.** This is the assumption that a central, exclusive, romantic relationship is the ultimate goal of adult life, and that it is therefore inherently more important than any other kind of connection.

It's the silent force that automatically places a two-year marriage above a twenty-year friendship in the social hierarchy. It's the cultural script that makes you feel like you are failing if your deepest, most life-sustaining bond is with a sibling or a best friend instead of a romantic partner.

THE CORE LIES OF THE OLD RULEBOOK

When you combine mononormativity and amatonormativity, you get the Monogamy Mindset in its full force: a script that teaches us that a single romantic partner should be the sun around which our entire life orbits. This script operates on a set of toxic, unexamined assumptions.

- It teaches us that love is a finite resource that can only be given to one person at a time.

- It insists that exclusivity is the ultimate proof of love, a sign that we are truly valued.

- It frames emotional distress as a sign the relationship is broken or that we are personally flawed.

- Most critically, it sells the dangerous belief that true security comes from controlling our partner's life and affections.

At its worst, this mindset justifies treating partners like property. It fuels controlling scripts, often without us realizing it. You may have even said or felt it yourself: "If you really loved me, you would…"

This isn't always a conscious attempt to manipulate. For many of us, it's the only tool we were ever given to ask for security. The no-bullshit reality is that each of these assumptions is built on a foundation of fear, not love.

HOW THE MONOGAMY MINDSET SHOWS UP IN REAL LIFE

Once you can see the pillars of the Old Rulebook, you start to see its symptoms everywhere. Two of the most common are the Relationship Escalator and Couple Privilege.

Table 2.1: The Monogamy Mindset vs. The No-Bullshit Reality

Old Script (The Monogamy Mindset)	No-Bullshit Reality
"True love means exclusivity."	Love is not a proof-of-ownership contract. It's possible to love multiple people deeply.
"If you loved me, you wouldn't want anyone else."	Desire for others doesn't negate love for you. These feelings can coexist.
"Emotional distress means something is wrong with the relationship."	Emotional distress is a smoke alarm, not a moral verdict. It signals a need, not a flaw.
"We're only serious if we're moving toward marriage or merging lives."	Commitment can take many forms. Relationship success isn't one-size-fits-all.
"My partner should meet all my needs."	No one person can be your everything—and that's not a failure, it's reality.
"Control = security."	Security comes from trust, not restriction. Control breeds fear, not safety.
"The couple comes first—everyone else adjusts."	All partners deserve voice and respect. "Opening up" means opening to shared humanity.

Symptom 1: The Relationship Escalator

Coined by author and activist Amy Gahran, the Relationship Escalator is society's standard, linear path for "successful" relationships: dating, exclusivity, moving in, merging finances, marriage, and children. Deviating from this path is seen as failure. This model makes longevity the ultimate prize, teaching us that a relationship's worth is measured by its duration rather than its health. Ethical non-monogamy invites you to get off the escalator and design connections based on what actually nourishes you.

Symptom 2: Couple Privilege

Even when a couple opens up, the monogamy mindset often persists as Couple Privilege. This is the unspoken social and emotional advantage held by the established couple, which marginalizes other partners unless actively dismantled.

In real life, couple privilege feels like:

1. Being the person whose schedule is always expected to be the most flexible.

2. Your relationship being treated as a fun hobby while theirs is the "real" one.

3. The couple making major decisions without consulting other partners.

4. A new partner being summarily dismissed (via a veto) if they become inconvenient.

Unlearning this means seeing new partners as whole people with equal stakes in the relational ecosystem, not as temporary guests you can send home at will.

Case Study: The Birthday Blunder

Jen has been dating a married couple, Mark and Lisa, for six months. When her birthday comes up, she's excited to spend it with them.

When she brings it up, Mark says, "Oh, we'd love to, but that's our regular Friday game night with our college friends. It's just… it's a whole thing to explain you, so we can't really miss it. We can totally do dinner on Saturday, though!"

The message, however unintentional, is clear: Jen's milestone is a flexible event, while the couple's established social routine is a non-negotiable priority. This isn't a failure of scheduling; it's a failure to see Jen as an equal stakeholder in the relational ecosystem, a classic symptom of unexamined couple privilege. This is a common blind spot, often unintentional, born from the old rulebook. The work is not to blame Mark, but for him to recognize the impact and learn to write a new script.

From Unconscious Programming to Conscious Choice

The goal of this exploration is not to reject everything you've learned in monogamous relationships, many of which offer profound lessons in commitment and intimacy. The goal is to **discern**. It's to sort through the tools you've been given and decide which ones truly serve you, and which are simply part of an inherited script you never agreed to follow. The work is moving from unconscious programming to conscious choice.

PAUSE AND CONSIDER

- When you feel jealous or threatened, what is the first story your mind jumps to? Is it rooted in a fear of scarcity, a need for control, or a comparison to others?

- What does the word "commitment" mean to you if you remove sexual exclusivity from the equation? What specific behaviors demonstrate this kind of commitment?

- What is one small, concrete action you can take this week to build security from within yourself, rather than seeking it from controlling a partner's behavior?

NO-BULLSHIT TL;DR

- The Monogamy Mindset is the set of inherited cultural scripts we all learn. This is a critique of the default system, not the personal choice of monogamy.

- Key scripts—like the Relationship Escalator and Couple Privilege—automatically center the couple and can harm other relationships if left unexamined.

- Seeing these scripts is the first step. The work is not to reject everything you've learned, but to question which parts truly serve you and your partners.

- The goal is to move from unconscious programming to conscious choice, building relationships that are authentically yours.

CHAPTER 3: A TOUR OF THE ENM LANDSCAPE

GUT-CHECKING POLYAMORY, SWINGING, OPEN RELATIONSHIPS, AND MORE

You've begun to question the old, inherited rulebook, and now you're looking at the vast, sprawling landscape of Ethical Non-Monogamy.

This landscape offers a dazzling–and perhaps overwhelming– variety of relationship styles. Some will feel familiar; others will be completely new. This tour covers the most common styles of ENM, exploring their core philosophies, their values, and their common pitfalls. It is to help you understand what's being offered so you can figure out what might actually fit your life. Think of this as a tour of the philosophies. Later, we'll explore the physical spaces where these communities gather– from social clubs to swingers' resorts to kink dungeons–and show you how to navigate each one safely.

Pay close attention to your own reactions as we go. Your gut feelings are your best guide to what might genuinely work for you.

A CRITICAL WARNING: LABELS ARE TOOLS, NOT CAGES

As we explore these styles, you'll encounter a lot of labels: hierarchical polyamory, solo poly, swinger, relationship anarchist. It's tempting, especially when you feel lost and grasping for a sense of identity, to grab the first label that sounds right and cling to it like a life raft.

Resist this urge.

Labels are useful shorthand. They are pointers. They help us find other people who might share our values and quickly describe a complex set of agreements. But they are tools, not identities. They are a starting point for a conversation, not the conversation itself.

The danger is when a label becomes a rigid box, a new dogma to replace the old one. You start trying to contort your real, evolving feelings to fit the label, rather than letting the label simply describe your reality. If you define yourself as a hierarchical polyamorist, you might refuse to see when a so-called secondary relationship is becoming more central to your life. If you insist you're "just a swinger," you might deny the very real and terrifying romantic feelings you're developing for a regular play partner, forcing them into a toxic secret.

Use these labels to help you understand the landscape and articulate what you want. But hold them loosely. Your relationships, in all their messy, evolving reality, should define the label—not the other way around.

STYLE 1: POLYAMORY

- **The What:** A relationship practice centered on having, or being open to having, multiple emotionally intimate, romantic relationships simultaneously.

- **The Core Idea:** Love is an infinite resource, not a zero-sum game. The goal is to build multiple, deep, emotionally authentic connections, and to manage the finite realities of time and energy with integrity.

- **The Bullshit Zone:** The "Polyer-Than-Thou" complex, where non-monogamy is worn as a badge of moral superiority; turning one partner into an unpaid therapist for another relationship; or letting the addictive high of a new romance burn down the trust of an established partnership.

- **Ethical Practice Demands:** High emotional intelligence, impeccable time and energy management, and radical personal responsibility for your own feelings.

GUT CHECK: IS POLYAMORY FOR YOU?

Imagine this. It's 10 p.m. on a Wednesday. Your partner of five years, who was supposed to be home an hour ago from a date with their new partner of three months, sends you a text:

"Having an amazing time with Alex. We're talking about grabbing dessert, so I'm going to be home later than I thought. Don't wait up!"

Check your gut. What is your immediate, visceral reaction?

1. A genuine warmth spreads through your chest. You're so happy they're connecting deeply. You send back a

supportive message and go to sleep peacefully, feeling secure and full of love.

2. A flicker of annoyance about the time, mixed with a small pang of envy, but overall, you're genuinely glad they're happy. You can deal with the small stuff tomorrow.

3. A cold knot forms in your stomach. Your brain generates a highlight reel of all the ways this new person is better than you. You spend the next three hours doomscrolling their social media.

4. Full-blown panic. This feels like an abandonment. You feel replaced and furious. You start typing a long, angry text message detailing every way they've failed you.

Analysis: There is no right answer, only your honest one. A mix of these reactions is normal. The goal is to find your emotional center of gravity. Does a feeling of warmth and security ultimately outweigh the fear and insecurity? Or does the panic and feeling of being replaced drown out everything else? If the dominant feeling is one of profound threat, that isn't a sign of failure. It is crucial data, likely an echo of the "Monogamy Mindset" that taught us a partner's new connection is a direct threat to our own. Your compass is working perfectly; it's telling you that this specific style might be a painful fit.

STYLE 2: SWINGING

Let's be clear from the start: Swinging is absolutely a form of Ethical Non-Monogamy. In some corners of the ENM world, there can be a subtle bias that treats relationship-focused polyamory as more "evolved" than sex-focused swinging. That is bullshit. The only thing that makes any practice "ethical" is the commitment to consent, honesty, and mutual respect. Swinging, when done with this integrity, is a valid, powerful, and deeply rewarding way to practice non-monogamy.

- **The What:** A practice, typically couple-centric, focused on sharing recreational sexual experiences to enhance a primary relationship, often within a community known as "The Lifestyle."

- **The Core Idea:** A shared adventure for a committed couple. The goal is to explore sexuality and novelty *together*, bringing that energy and excitement back into the primary relationship.

- **The Bullshit Zone:** One partner being subtly (or not-so-subtly) pressured into participating; treating other people— especially single women—as disposable props for a couple's fantasy; and rigid, controlling rules born from insecurity, not safety.

- **Ethical Practice Demands:** Enthusiastic, mutual desire from everyone involved; impeccable debriefing and aftercare; and a firm commitment to humanizing every single person you play with.

Gut Check: Is Swinging for You?

Imagine this. You and your partner are at a well-run, sexy house party. The music is a low thrum, the lighting is dim, and the air is thick with possibility. After chatting with another couple, you all move to a playroom. You watch your partner, just a few feet away, lean in and kiss someone new. It's not a polite peck; it's deep, hungry, and full of mutual desire. Your partner's eyes are closed; they are clearly lost in the moment.

Check your gut. What is your immediate, visceral reaction?

1. A jolt of electric heat. Watching your partner experience that much pleasure is a massive turn-on for you. You feel a surge of excitement and vicarious joy (compersion).

2. A tangled knot of nervousness and arousal. It's a little scary but also undeniably hot. You feel a bit insecure, but you're also eager to start your own exploration.

3. A cold wave of "mine" washes over you. Your brain is screaming, "That's my person. What's happening?" You feel possessive and deeply uncomfortable.

4. A complete emotional shutdown. You feel disconnected from your body, like you're watching a movie you don't want to be in. You want to go home. Immediately.

Analysis: There is no right answer, only your honest one. It's completely normal to feel both aroused and terrified. The question is about the balance. Is the excitement stronger than the possessiveness? Or does the feeling of violation completely overwhelm any sense of arousal? Pay attention to your body's deepest response. If the core feeling is one of deep-seated discomfort, that is not a flaw in your character. It is your nervous system giving you a clear signal that the visual reality of this style may be a hard limit for you.

STYLE 3: OPEN RELATIONSHIPS

- **The What**: A broad category where a committed couple creates a custom agreement that allows for some form of sexual and/or romantic connection with others.

- **The Core Idea**: A custom renovation project for a committed relationship. It acknowledges that love and commitment aren't tied to sexual exclusivity, allowing partners to design their own unique blueprint for connection.

- **The Bullshit Zone**: Vague agreements where "open" means something different to each person; the naive and doomed attempt to legislate emotions with a "no feelings" rule; and the central ethical failure of treating other people as disposable tools for the primary couple's personal growth.

- **Ethical Practice Demands**: Brutal specificity in your agreements, and a pre-negotiated plan for what to do when feelings inevitably arise.

Gut Check: Is an Open Relationship for You?

Imagine this. You and your partner have an agreement that you can have casual sexual encounters, but you've agreed to a strict "no feelings" rule. One night, your partner comes home from a date looking shaken. They sit you down and say:

"I messed up. I think I'm catching feelings for my new play partner. I know this is the one rule we had, and I'm so scared I've broken everything. I needed to tell you right away."

29

Check your gut. What is your immediate, visceral reaction?

1. Your first thought is, "Okay, we have a problem to solve together. Thank you for telling me." You feel a surge of compassion mixed with anxiety, but your primary concern is for your partner and your team.

2. You feel a flash of hurt followed by pragmatism. You're not thrilled, but you appreciate the honesty. You think, "This is what our 'feelings plan' was for. Let's talk about our options."

3. A hot wave of betrayal. Your mind screams, *"You broke the rule!"* You feel like they've cheated, and your first impulse is to demand they end the other connection immediately.

4. Complete and total panic. The "no feelings" rule was the only thing making you feel safe, and now the floor has crumbled beneath you. You feel you cannot trust them at all.

Analysis: There is no right answer, only your honest one. A "no feelings" rule is a bomb waiting to go off; your reaction to the explosion is the critical data. Does your mind frame this as a problem to solve collaboratively, or as a betrayal to be punished? If your security is fundamentally tied to the ability to control your partner's emotions, this isn't a personal failing-it's a sign of a deeply ingrained survival strategy. It suggests the inherent ambiguity of many open relationships may be a poor and painful fit for you right now.

STYLE 4: SOLO POLYAMORY & RELATIONSHIP ANARCHY

- **The What**: A radical rejection of the default social scripts. These are philosophies for people who are their own primary partner, building a life centered on autonomy.

- **The Core Idea**: To get off the Relationship Escalator entirely. It's about building a constellation of meaningful connections-romantic, platonic, or otherwise-without forcing them into a hierarchy or a pre-defined box.

- **The Bullshit Zone**: Using "autonomy" as a high-minded excuse for being a flake; confusing radical independence with emotional unavailability; and the performance of being so "evolved" that you refuse to make any clear agreements at all.

- **Ethical Practice Demands**: Radical self-responsibility, a fierce commitment to explicit communication, and the courage to build every single relationship from scratch.

Gut Check: Are Solo Polyamory or Relationship Anarchy for You?

Imagine this. You have been in a wonderful, loving relationship for a year with someone you adore. They are everything you've ever wanted in a partner. One day, you bring up the idea of moving in together in the next year or so. They take a deep breath and say:

"I love you more than I can say, and I am deeply committed to building a life with you. But I need you to hear me and believe me when I say this: I will never live with a partner. My home is my sanctuary. My commitment to you doesn't depend on a shared address."

Check your gut. What is your immediate, visceral reaction?

- A profound sense of relief. You feel the exact same way and are thrilled they said it first. The idea of maintaining your own home while having a deep, committed love feels like the ultimate freedom.

- Curiosity and a little disappointment. You had pictured cohabitation, but you're willing to explore what commitment looks like without it. Their need for autonomy doesn't feel like a rejection of you.

- A deep sense of hurt and rejection. Your immediate thought is, "If they really loved me, they would want this. This means they're not as serious about me as I am about them."

- A feeling of instability, like the ground has disappeared beneath you. To you, a relationship that isn't moving up the traditional Relationship Escalator feels directionless and fundamentally insecure.

Analysis: There is no right answer, only your honest one. This scenario directly tests your attachment to the Relationship Escalator. Does the idea of merging lives feel like a comforting goal or a terrifying cage? If the traditional milestones of cohabitation and marriage are a deep source of security and meaning for you, that is valid. Acknowledging this isn't admitting defeat; it's an act of profound self-awareness. These more independent paths would likely feel profoundly unsatisfying, and your compass is right to steer you away from them.

A FINAL WORD: THESE ARE STARTING POINTS, NOT RIGID BOXES

We've spent this chapter drawing clear lines between polyamory, swinging, open relationships, and relationship anarchy. We did this for one reason: to give you a clear vocabulary and a framework for understanding your own desires. If you don't know the difference between wanting emotional intimacy and wanting recreational sex, it is difficult to have an honest conversation with yourself or your partners.

The real world is far messier. These styles aren't mutually exclusive; they are ingredients you can combine to create your own unique relational recipe.

- A polyamorous couple might also love going to swinger clubs for casual play (Polyswingers).

- A solo polyamorist might have a deeply romantic partner and also a casual, open-relationship-style connection.

- A relationship anarchist might find that one of their connections organically evolves into something that looks a lot like a primary partnership, even if they don't use the label.

The purpose of this tour was not to force you into a box. It was to give you the language to understand the different kinds of connections that are possible. Use these words as tools to have better conversations. Take what serves you, combine it in a way that feels authentic, and leave the rest. The only "right" way is the one you and your partners co-create with honesty and consent.

NO-BULLSHIT TL;DR

- ENM is not a single path but a diverse landscape of philosophies and styles.

- There is no "best" style. The only right choice is the one that is honest, consensual, and sustainable for you and your partners.

- Your gut reactions are an important guide. The "Gut Check" scenarios are designed to help you listen to your own truth, not what you think you should feel.

- Labels are tools, not cages. Your chosen style describes your current agreements, not a permanent identity. You are always allowed to evolve.

CHAPTER 4: THIS WASN'T MY IDEA

A GUIDE FOR THE PARTNER ON THE OTHER SIDE

This may be the only chapter in this book that you read.

Perhaps you're here because the person you built a life with just sat you down at the kitchen table and detonated your world.

The delivery is rarely gentle. The conversation that changes everything often starts as a clumsy monologue because, let's be honest, no one ever taught them how to have it. It can be a storm of pseudo-enlightened therapy-speak, where your partner announces they must "honor their truth," with little regard for the shrapnel hitting you. It can be a blunt, brutal confession: "I've fallen in love with someone else. I'm sorry."

Or it can be a cascade of fumbled words that don't even make sense-a terrified vomiting of a truth they can no longer hold inside, followed by a silence that feels louder than any scream.

Whatever the words, the result is the same: the ground gives way beneath you.

The shock is more than an emotion; it's a physical event. You can't get enough air. Sounds become distant. You might find yourself staring at a saltshaker or a crack in the wall—anything to anchor you to a reality that is rapidly dissolving.

And in the days that follow, the grief can be an all-consuming fog. It's not a tidy sadness; it's a full-body experience. It's the sudden, uncontrollable sobbing while you're driving. It's the feeling of being a ghost in your own life, performing normal tasks while a storm rages inside you.

If you are in that place right now-if your world has been shattered by a conversation you never asked to have-this chapter is for you. Your feelings are not an overreaction. They are a normal, human response to a profound loss. Before we talk about tools or ethics, we have to sit with you, right here in the rubble, and acknowledge the validity of your pain.

You are likely feeling a tidal wave of emotions. It might feel like:

- **Grieving** the relationship you thought you had. That loss is real, and it is valid.

- **Terrified** of losing your partner, your family, and the future you planned together.

- **Furious** that the life you were carefully cultivating is being threatened and disrupted.

- Asking yourself, over and over, "**Am I not enough**?"

Again, none of this is an overreaction. It is a logical response to a seismic shift in your life.

The No-Bullshit Truth of Your Position

You are now at a crossroads, and you have agency here. Your partner may have initiated this conversation, but you are an equal participant in what happens next. Here are some foundational truths to hold onto:

- **"No" is a complete and valid answer.** You do not have to agree to this. You are allowed to say, "I love you, but I cannot be in a non-monogamous relationship. That is my boundary." This is not an ultimatum; it is a statement of your core needs. Your partner then has a choice to make, but you are not obligated to abandon your own fundamental requirements for a relationship.

- **This is a negotiation, not a verdict.** Your partner has stated a desire. This is the beginning of a conversation, not the end of one. You get to have your own needs, fears, and boundaries heard and respected.

- **Your timeline is your own**. You may be pressured to "get on board" quickly. You are allowed to say, "I need time. I need to process this. I need us to go to therapy. I am not ready to make any decisions right now."

- **You are not broken for wanting monogamy.** Don't let anyone-especially people in some ENM communities who should know better-tell you that you need to be "more evolved." Choosing a monogamous structure is a valid, powerful, and respectable decision. It is not a sign that you are "possessive" or "insecure."

This book is a tool for you, regardless of the path you choose from here.

But what if, after acknowledging all of that, a small, quiet part of you is still curious? What if you want to understand, not just to appease them, but for yourself? If you feel a pull not just to say "no," but to explore-even if it's just exploring your own thoughts and feelings-then the rest of these pages can help.

Even if you ultimately decide to reject non-monogamy, this book can equip you to navigate this impossible conversation with agency, understand the language your partner is using, and give you a framework for clarifying and holding your own non-negotiable boundaries.

You did not ask for this journey, but you are on it now. Your first responsibility is to be honest with yourself about what you truly want and need. You are a whole person in this dynamic, not an obstacle to your partner's desires.

NO-BULLSHIT TL;DR

- Your feelings are a compass, not a flaw. Your world just exploded; your grief, fear, and anger are pointing toward the truth.

- You hold the power of "no." Your partner does not get to make this decision without you.

- You are not on their timeline. You are allowed to say, "I need time." Full stop.

- Monogamy is a valid choice, not a moral failing. You are not less "evolved" for wanting it.

- Your needs are not an obstacle. They are a non-negotiable part of this conversation.

CHAPTER 5: THE INHERITED SCRIPT

DISMANTLING THE MYTH OF THE "ONE RIGHT WAY"

If you've ever felt a pull toward connection outside of your relationship-and then felt a hot, sickening wave of shame for it-this chapter is for you. If you've ever wondered if you're somehow broken for not finding lifelong, sexually exclusive monogamy to be a perfect, seamless fit, this chapter is your permission slip to stop blaming yourself.

Because that feeling isn't a personal flaw. It's a glitch in the system.

You're running ancient, human hardware—a brain and body forged over 200,000 years of interdependent survival. But you've been forced to run software that's only a few thousand years old: the inherited script of Lifelong, Sexually-Exclusive, Romantic Monogamy.

This chapter is about understanding that the software was never designed for your happiness. It was designed to solve a business problem and was later supercharged with religious dogma. Knowing this dismantles the myth that there is only one "right" way to be human, and frees you to ask a more interesting question.

HUMANITY'S OLDEST STORY: THE COMMUNAL WEB

For the vast majority of our time on this planet—over 95% of it—we lived as nomadic hunter-gatherers. Our social instincts were forged in that world, where an isolated two-person couple was often a death sentence. Survival depended on a web of robust, interdependent bonds.

This isn't just theory. Let's be specific with two well-documented examples.

- Among the **Mosuo** of China, the foundational social and economic unit is the stable **matrilineal household**, run by a senior woman. Romantic and sexual relationships, known as "walking marriages," exist separately from this core unit. A man will visit his partner at night but returns to his own mother's household, which remains his primary home and responsibility.
- For the **Canela** of Brazil, the belief in **partible paternity**—that a child can have multiple biological fathers—is a sophisticated social strategy. It is believed that contributions of semen from several men build a stronger fetus. More importantly, this practice creates a broad and resilient web of kinship, formally obligating multiple fathers to care for and protect the child.

These are not "primitive" arrangements; they are intelligent social technologies for building stable families and communities. It's also crucial to remember that these are living cultures, not historical relics, and they continue to adapt in the modern world.

THE GREAT MONOGAMY IMPOSITION

So what changed? A powerful one-two punch that reshaped human society.

The first blow was economic. The Agricultural Revolution introduced private property, which created an unromantic problem: inheritance. How could a man ensure his land passed only to his legitimate heirs? Enforceable monogamy for women was the business solution—a script for protecting property.

But a script for property is not enough to control a human heart. For that, you need a more powerful tool: morality.

This is where the rise of major world religions delivered the second, more powerful blow. They took an economic arrangement and recoded it as divine law. Suddenly, straying wasn't just a threat to inheritance; it was a sin, a stain on your immortal soul. This religious framework was revolutionary because it established a set of strict, unwavering rules and claimed they were not a social construct, but a universal, unchanging truth, straight from God.

This is the source of the deep, often unexamined guilt that so many of us feel. It's the cognitive dissonance of your human nature clashing with a rule you've been told is absolute. This is why a simple desire can feel like a profound moral failing.

The result was a powerful combination: an economic system built on property, reinforced by a moral code built on guilt. This code was then spread globally, often through the force of colonial powers who used it to dismantle other ways of life.

A CRITICAL WARNING: THE SMUG ANTI-MONOGAMIST

As you explore this history, let's call out some bullshit you will encounter in ENM spaces. You will meet someone who, with an air of smug superiority, declares that monogamy is "unnatural and wrong." They'll use the facts we just discussed as a weapon to pathologize a valid way of life.

Do not fall for it. This book is not an argument that monogamy is wrong.

An ethical life has nothing to do with the number of partners you have. It has everything to do with how you treat them. Monogamy, practiced with honesty, trust, and mutual respect, can be a profoundly ethical and beautiful way to build a life. A polyamorous relationship built on manipulation and selfishness is an unethical dumpster fire. "Ethical" is about conduct, not structure.

So Where Does This Leave You?

It leaves you standing in an open field, free from the cage of the one "right" way.

You now know that the rules you were taught are not timeless truths. They are historical artifacts. This knowledge is liberating, but it's also destabilizing. If there is no single, correct map from the outside world-not from history, not from religion, not from society-then where do you find your direction?

Freedom without a compass is just another word for being lost. To move forward, you can no longer look to the external world for answers. You must look inward. You have to build your own map—and to do that, you first need to forge your own compass.

NO-BULLSHIT TL;DR

- The monogamy you were taught is not a timeless, biological truth; it's a relatively recent script written for property and enforced by religious dogma.

- Your "conflicting feelings" aren't a sign you're broken; they're a normal response to an inherited script that doesn't fit everyone.

- "Ethical" is about your conduct, not your relationship structure. Monogamy is a valid and powerful choice when practiced with integrity.

- Understanding this history is not about finding a better model in the past; it's about freeing yourself from the authority of any single script so you can make a conscious choice.

PART 2: THE CORE TOOLKIT

CHAPTER 6: YOUR PERSONAL COMPASS

A PRACTICAL GUIDE TO KNOWING WHAT YOU WANT

You've explored the landscape and questioned the old, inherited scripts. Now comes the most important, and often most difficult, work: asking yourself a simple, terrifying question:

What do I actually want?

This chapter is not about creating a rigid checklist for a "perfect" partner. It is about starting the practical, messy work of forging your personal compass. This compass doesn't point to a single, fixed "true north"; it's a snapshot of your internal world *right now*. It is a tool to help you understand your own direction so you can communicate more clearly with the people you care about.

It's okay if you're confused. It's okay if what you want today is different from what you wanted last year, or what you might want next year. This is not a test to find your one "true" self. It is a gentle investigation to create a starting point for the ongoing conversation you will have with your partners and with yourself.

THE NO-BULLSHIT TRUTH ABOUT CHOICE AND COMPROMISE

Let's start by dismantling a core myth of romantic love: the idea that you will find one person who meets all your needs or that you should become the one person who meets all of theirs.

Here's the no-bullshit truth: Every relationship involves compromise. You are making concessions to be with them, and they are making concessions to be with you. Because no one is anyone's everything. One of the most profound gifts of ENM is that it gives you explicit permission to stop demanding that one person be the source of all your happiness—and to release yourself from the impossible burden of being theirs.

The goal of this chapter is not to build a list of demands. It is to gain enough self-clarity to have an honest conversation with a potential or current partner about where your wants align, where they differ, and what you might be able to build together. Helping a partner stretch is a gift; asking them to perform is a recipe for misery. This is about finding genuine compatibility, not just a willingness to perform.

PART 1: AN INVESTIGATION INTO YOUR WANTS AND NEEDS

Let's begin with a broad exploration. We're not looking for definitive labels yet, just clues. This is about noticing what feels good and what feels bad so you can start to sketch a map of your internal world. To help you get started, here is a spectrum of common wants and needs people discover in relationships. Read through them and notice what resonates with you right now.

A Spectrum of Relational Wants & Needs

- **For Security:** Do you want predictability, clear agreements, and a sense of "coming home"? Or do you thrive on spontaneity and less defined structures?

- **For Autonomy:** Do you need significant time alone, separate friends, and the freedom to make decisions independently? Or do you prefer a more merged life with shared activities and decisions?

- **For Honesty:** Do you prefer radical transparency where everything is on the table? Or a "need-to-know" basis that respects each person's privacy?

- **For Intimacy:** Does intimacy for you mean deep emotional conversations? Frequent physical touch? Shared intellectual projects? All of the above?

- **For Growth:** Are you looking for partners who challenge you to grow and evolve? Or are you seeking a more comfortable, stable connection at this stage of your life?

- **For Community:** Is it important that your partners are integrated into your social life? Or do you prefer to keep your relationships in separate, distinct boxes?

- **For Playfulness:** Are you looking for fun, lighthearted, and adventurous connections? Or are you seeking something more serious and settled?

Now, let's get personal.

Exploration A: Your Relational Highs and Lows

Think about the connections in your life—romantic, platonic, or familial. Bring to mind a time you felt deeply happy, safe, or seen in a relationship. What was happening? What need was being met? Was it a moment of thrilling adventure or quiet security?

Now, think of a time you felt hurt, drained, or misunderstood. What was missing? Was it a lack of respect? A feeling of being controlled and having no autonomy?

Exploration B: Your Curiosities and Experiments

One of the core tenets of this path is exploration. You may not know what you want until you try it. What are you curious about? What have you always wondered about but never experienced? (e.g., "I'm curious about what a kink dynamic would feel like.")

What have you tried that you thought you'd like but didn't? (e.g., "I thought I wanted a big, kitchen-table polycule, but I tried it and found it exhausting.") It's okay to discover you don't like something. That's not failure; that's data.

PART 2: FORGING YOUR CORE VALUES AND GUIDING PRINCIPLES

Now that you've explored your general wants, let's distill them into a more focused tool. The patterns you just uncovered point toward your Core Values—the three to five themes that are most essential for your well-being in a relationship at this stage of your life.

Reflect on the themes that feel most significant to you in relationships–such as Security, Autonomy, Honesty, Growth, or Playfulness. Choose the three to five values that resonate most strongly at this stage of your life.

A value is an idea; a Guiding Principle is a commitment that brings that value to life. The next step is to turn each chosen value into a clear principle for yourself, making your intentions actionable and meaningful.

The "Fear vs. Intention" Exercise

For each of your chosen Core Values, ask yourself: "When I feel insecure about this, what is the controlling demand I am tempted to impose on someone else?" This isn't a sign that you're a bad person; it's a sign that you're human. Fear speaks in the language of the old rulebook, trying to find safety through control. Frame it as a "You must…" or "You can't…" statement. This is your fear talking.

Now, flip that fear-based demand into a personal principle for yourself. This should be an "I will…" statement about your own actions.

This set of guiding principles forms the core of your personal compass. It's a tool for navigating your own choices with integrity. But a principle is just a theory. The next step is putting it into practice with the most important person in your life: yourself.

Table 6.1: From Values to Principles

A tool for transforming fears into guiding relational commitments.

Core Value	Fear-Based Demand ("You must...")	Guiding Principle ("I will...")
Security	You must tell me everything the moment it happens.	I will communicate my needs calmly and allow space for their process.
Autonomy	You can't make plans without checking with me first.	I will honor their independence and manage my reactions responsibly.
Honesty	You must never hide anything from me—even your feelings.	I will create an environment where honesty is safe and welcomed.
Playfulness	You must always be up for fun, or I'll feel unwanted.	I will bring levity without making it someone else's responsibility.
Growth	You can't be with someone who challenges you more than I do.	I will focus on my own evolution and support theirs without comparison.

PART 3: YOUR FIRST AGREEMENT IS WITH YOURSELF

Before you can make a trustworthy agreement with a partner, you must first learn to make and keep agreements with yourself. This is the foundation of all relational integrity. Part of growing up—in life and in this way of relating—is the practice of creating your own internal rules and evolving them into deeply held agreements.

This is critical because, as you've probably noticed, we are all terrible at guessing how we will feel about something in the future. We can theorize all day, but we don't know what an experience will actually feel like until we're in it. This is why we need to practice with ourselves first.

Let's clearly distinguish between an Internal Rule and an Internal Agreement:

- **Internal Rule:** Think of this as a conscious, self-imposed guardrail. You're creating a temporary rule to manage an impulse because your head and your gut aren't on the same page yet. Following an Internal Rule often requires deliberate effort and self-discipline.

    Example: You're new to ENM and notice anxiety when viewing your metamour's social media. You set an internal rule: "I will not look at my metamour's social media profiles," even though you're still tempted. It's an intentional restraint you're imposing until you feel more secure.

- **Internal Agreement:** This is what happens when the guardrail comes down because you no longer need it. Your values and your authentic desires have aligned. It feels effortless because it is.

    Example: After months of practicing ENM, you notice you genuinely no longer feel the urge to check your metamour's social media. You now have an internal agreement: "I don't check their profiles because I trust my relationship and respect their privacy." This isn't forced; it's simply how you authentically feel and act.

Think of an Internal Rule as a training wheel—temporary support as you build strength and stability. Eventually, as your emotional muscles strengthen, you naturally transition from needing a rule to having an internal agreement. This shift indicates real growth and self-integration.

The Ultimate Litmus Test

Your ability to follow through on the rules and agreements you make with yourself is the single best predictor of whether you will be able to keep them with other people.

If you tell yourself, "I'm going to go to the gym three times this week," and you consistently don't, that is data.

If you promise yourself, "I will not text my ex," and you do it anyway, that is data.

This isn't about shaming yourself. It's about radical self-honesty. Think of your follow-through with yourself as a private, gentle litmus test for your own integrity. If you can't trust yourself to honor your own stated intentions, why should a partner trust you with their heart?

Before you can be a safe harbor for someone else, you must first become a trustworthy navigator of your own ship. The work isn't to be perfect. It's to practice. Start with small, achievable promises to yourself. Build a track record of self-trust.

Because you cannot safely ask for someone else's heart until you can trust yourself with your own.

PAUSE AND CONSIDER

- Recall the last promise you made only to yourself. Be brutally honest: did you keep it? What does your track record with your own integrity tell you about your current readiness to make high-stakes agreements with others?

- Look at the "Guiding Principles" you developed. Which one feels the most natural to you? Which one will require the most conscious practice?

- What is one small, achievable promise you can make—and keep—to yourself this week to build self-trust?

NO-BULLSHIT TL;DR

- Knowing what you want isn't selfish; it's the foundation for ethical relationships. Start by getting honest with yourself.

- No one can be your everything, and you are not meant to be theirs. The goal is to find compromises that feel authentic, not resentful.

- Turn your fears into principles. Use the "Fear vs. Intention" exercise to transform anxiety into actionable, personal commitments.

- Your first and most important agreements are with yourself. Building self-trust is a practice, and it's the bedrock of all healthy connections.

CHAPTER 7: LOVE, TIME, & ENERGY

THE FINITE REALITIES OF INFINITE LOVE

You might have infinite love, but you only have 24 hours in a day. This is the fundamental, non-negotiable conflict of practicing non-monogamy.

The poets and greeting card companies have sold us a beautiful lie: that love is all you need. Polyamory, in its own way, echoes part of this by teaching us that love itself isn't a finite resource. This is a profound and liberating truth.

But here is the no-bullshit, iron-clad law of the universe:

Love may be infinite, but you are not.

Time is not infinite.

Energy is not.

Emotional bandwidth is not.

Money is not.

THE MYTH OF ENDLESS CAPACITY & THE GOSPEL OF "ABUNDANCE"

If you've been in ENM or spiritual communities long enough, you've probably heard someone say something like:

"I don't believe in scarcity. I operate from a place of abundance. I have room for everyone."

That sounds beautiful, enlightened, and deeply spiritual. And the person saying it often genuinely means well. They are often repeating a script from spiritual communities that values infinite openness above all else. But without being grounded in the reality of our finite bodies and schedules, it can be a prelude to a catastrophic burnout that leaves a trail of neglected partners and broken promises in its wake. This belief doesn't translate to a mandate that your sexuality must be infinitely available. You do not have to have sex with everyone to prove you believe love is infinite. That is not a demonstration of enlightened abundance; it is often a performance rooted in a misunderstanding of what these concepts actually mean.

When you hear someone preach this gospel of "abundance," ask yourself a simple question: Whose abundance are they spending? Often, it is the abundance of other people's emotional labor, time, and flexibility. Love without logistics isn't abundance. It is irresponsibility disguised in a spiritual vocabulary.

THE NRE VS. ERE FALLACY: THE DANGER OF COMPARING A SPRINT TO A MARATHON

One of the most predictable and destructive traps in non-monogamy is comparing the energy of a new relationship to that of an established one.

New Relationship Energy (NRE) is a powerful, intoxicating neurochemical cocktail. It's novelty, infatuation, and idealization all rolled into one. It feels like boundless energy, effortless connection, and a storybook romance. It is also, by definition, temporary. It's a sprint.

Established Relationship Energy (ERE)—sometimes called Old Relationship Energy (ORE)—is what you have in a long-term partnership. It's the quiet, deep, and powerful energy of shared history, profound trust, and mutual understanding. It's knowing how your partner takes their coffee. It's the comfortable silence you can share. It's the shorthand language you've built over years. It is a marathon of quiet, steady connection.

The No-Bullshit Reality: A common failure mode is for a partner high on NRE to look at their established relationship and see it as boring or broken simply because it lacks the addictive fireworks of the new one. This isn't a moral failing; it's a predictable biological and psychological trap. The ethical challenge is to consciously choose to honor the quiet, life-sustaining sun of an established bond, even when the loud, hot bonfire of NRE is demanding all of your attention.

Table 7.1: Comparing NRE and ERE

Feature	New Relationship Energy (NRE)	Established Relationship Energy (ERE)
Core Feeling	Excitement, infatuation, intensity	Comfort, security, deep knowing
Energy Type	A high-intensity sprint	A long-distance marathon
Foundation	Novelty and idealization	Shared history and trust
Primary Risk	Impulsive decisions; neglect of existing commitments	Being taken for granted; stagnation if not tended

Ethical practice requires you to consciously honor the value of your established relationships, especially when you are high on NRE. It means proactively protecting time and energy for your long-term partners and refusing to engage in the unfair comparison game.

THE FINITE RESOURCES OF CONNECTION

When you engage in multiple relationships, you're not just spending love. You are managing a complex budget of several different, non-renewable resources. Getting honest about what you actually have to spend is step one. Below are the key relational currencies you must account for.

Table 7.2: The Finite Currencies of Connection

Relational Currency	What It Represents	Why It Matters
Time	The literal hours in your day to be with or communicate with someone	You can't be two places at once. Overcommitting leads to disconnection and burnout.
Energy	Your mental, emotional, and physical capacity to be present, attentive, and engaged	If you're exhausted, your presence suffers—even when you're physically there.
Attention	Your ability to focus and truly listen, understand, and respond	Split focus leads to misunderstandings and unmet needs.
Money	The financial cost of maintaining relationships (dates, travel, health care, etc.)	Financial stress adds hidden strain and can magnify resentment or inequity.
Logistical Bandwidth	The mental overhead of planning, scheduling, and coordinating a multi-person life	The more plates you're spinning, the more likely something gets dropped.
Self-Care Capacity	Time and energy left over to meet your own needs	Neglecting this leads to resentment, dysregulation, and eventual collapse.

AGREEMENTS AS AN ENERGY CONSERVATION TOOL

One of the biggest hidden costs in any relationship is decision fatigue. Every choice we make—from what to have for dinner to how to navigate a complex emotional situation—consumes our finite mental and emotional energy. This is where your agreements become one of your most powerful tools for resource management.

A good agreement automates a future decision. This is one of its most powerful and overlooked functions.

- **Without an agreement:** "My partner is out on a date. Should I text them? Will it bother them? Will I seem insecure if I do? Will I feel anxious if I don't?" This internal debate is a massive drain on your emotional battery.

- **With an agreement:** "Our agreement is that we send one 'goodnight' text. I will wait for that and trust the process." The decision is already made. The energy is conserved.

Clear, pre-negotiated structures don't limit freedom; they create it by reducing guesswork, conserving energy, and creating space for connection. When you have a clear agreement, you have taken a recurring question off the table and freed up the energy you would have spent debating it. This allows your nervous system to relax, knowing that the big safety questions have already been answered, freeing up your precious mental energy to focus on what actually matters: connecting, loving, and enjoying your partners.

Polysaturation: The Art of Knowing When You're Full

Polysaturation is the point at which you have reached your full capacity for maintaining meaningful relationships. Taking on anyone else would mean your well-being, and the health of your existing connections, would suffer. It is the relational equivalent of being full at a banquet. Even if that dessert looks amazing, eating it will make you sick.

Signs You Are At or Beyond Your Polysaturation Point

- You are constantly exhausted, irritable, or overwhelmed.

- All your partners (including yourself) feel perpetually neglected.

- You are always apologizing for being unavailable, distracted, or late.

- You have no time for solitude, hobbies, or non-relational friendships.

- Your health is suffering. You're not sleeping enough, eating well, or exercising.

- You feel like you're constantly in "crisis mode," just putting out the next fire.

IF YOU THINK IT'S GETTING LATE, IT ALREADY IS

Your body will tell you when you are overdoing it. Do not wait until you are completely drained, exhausted, and running on fumes to leave a date, a party, or other event. By then, it's too late. You've overdrawn your account, and you will pay for it the next day with fatigue, irritability, and a diminished capacity to show up for your other partners and responsibilities.

Honor that first whisper of "I should go." It is an act of profound self-care and a gift to your future self and all of your relationships.

NO-BULLSHIT TL;DR

- Love may be infinite, but you are not. Honoring your finite time, energy, and attention isn't a failure; it's the foundation of sustainable relationships.

- Beware the NRE hangover. Consciously protect and honor your established relationships, especially when a new connection feels intoxicating.

- Use clear agreements as an energy conservation tool. Automating decisions reduces fatigue and creates more space for connection.

- Learn your polysaturation point. Saying "no" to a new connection is more ethical than saying a "yes" to everyone and neglecting them all.

CHAPTER 8: THE UNF*CKABLE CONVERSATION

A SIMPLE, FOUR-STEP METHOD FOR TALKING ABOUT HARD THINGS

Let's be honest. Most of our difficult conversations are doomed before they even begin. They are doomed because they start with an accusation, a judgment, or a demand: "You always…," "You never…," "You make me feel…" The last one, often disguised as a question, is still an accusation: "So, I guess you just didn't want to see me last night?"

An accusation puts the other person on the defensive immediately. Their brain shuts down, their walls go up, and the chance for a real connection vanishes. The conversation is no longer about solving a problem together; it's about one person trying to win and the other trying to defend themselves. This isn't because we are bad people; it's because this is the only script we were ever taught for conflict. This is a recipe for resentment.

To have a conversation that actually works—one that is nearly impossible to fuck up—we need a different model. The most powerful tool for this is the four-step framework of Nonviolent Communication (NVC), developed by Dr. Marshall Rosenberg. At its core, the model is brilliant.

Frankly, a lot of the literature around it can feel dense, preachy, and bogged down in a kind of gentle-parenting language that can come across as shaming. This is the no-bullshit, stripped-down version, focused entirely on the practical mechanics of the tool.

THE UNF*CKABLE CONVERSATION FRAMEWORK

This is not a magic formula that will solve all your problems. It is a simple, practical framework for talking about hard things in a way that minimizes blame and maximizes the chance of being heard. It organizes the conversation into four distinct, intentional steps.

Step 1: The Observation (What Actually Happened)

Start with a neutral, objective fact—what a video camera could have recorded. It must be stripped of all interpretation, judgment, or assumptions about the other person's motives.

- **Instead of:** "You completely ignored me at the party last night." (This is a story about their intent.)
- **Try:** "When we were at the party last night, we didn't speak for the last hour." (This is an observable fact.)

Step 2: The Feeling (How It Felt to You)

Now, share your emotional reaction using an "I" statement. This is about your internal experience, not what they did to you.

- **Instead of:** "You made me feel abandoned." (This is blame disguised as a feeling.)
- **Try:** "I felt lonely and insecure." (This is an honest statement about your own feelings.)

Step 3: The Need (What You Actually Want)

This is the most crucial, and often most overlooked, step. Your feeling is a signal pointing to an unmet need. What is it? A need is a universal human requirement, like the need for security, connection, respect, or autonomy.

- **Instead of:** "I need you to pay more attention to me." (This is vague and sounds like a demand.)
- **Try:** "The need that came up for me was a need for connection and to feel prioritized." (This is a clear statement of an internal need.)

Step 4: The Request (A Specific, Actionable Ask)

Finally, make a clear, concrete, and doable request that would help meet your need. A true request is not a demand; the other person is free to say no, and your ask is the beginning of a negotiation.

- **Instead of:** "You need to be more considerate." (This is a vague demand for a personality change.)

- **Try:** "Would you be willing to check in with me every 30 minutes at a party?" (This is a specific, actionable request.)

PUTTING IT ALL TOGETHER: THE NO-BULLSHIT SCRIPT

When you put these four steps together, you get a simple, powerful script for having almost any difficult conversation:

"When I see/hear [1. The Observation], I feel [2. The Feeling] because I need [3. The Need]. Would you be willing to [4. The Request]?"

Examples in Action

- **Blamey Way:** "You never make time for me anymore; I am not important to you."

- **The No-Bullshit Way (Using the Script):** "When our last two date nights got cancelled, I felt hurt and pretty unimportant. I'm feeling disconnected, and I have a need to feel like we're on solid ground. Would you be willing to look at our calendars and schedule a dedicated, protected date night for next week?"

A CRITICAL WARNING: SPOTTING THE WEAPONIZED VERSION

This framework is a tool for connection, but any tool can be a weapon. In the hands of a manipulator, the structure of the Unf*ckable Conversation can be used to disguise an accusation as a vulnerable feeling. It can sound incredibly "conscious" and "evolved" while being deeply controlling.

Here is what the misuse looks like. Imagine a partner is feeling insecure about your date with someone else and wants to stop you from going:

- **The Weaponized Version:** "When you choose to go on your date tonight (Observation), I feel abandoned and unsafe (Feeling) because I have a need for security in our connection (Need). So, I'm requesting that you cancel your date to help me feel safe again (Request)."

Let's break down why this is bullshit, even though it follows the four-part structure. It's important to remember that people often do this when they are terrified and feel powerless—it's a clumsy attempt to get a core need met by controlling the situation. But even if the intention isn't malicious, the impact is still deeply harmful.

1. **The "Feeling" is a Judgment.** "Abandoned" isn't just a feeling; it's a story you are telling about the other person's actions (that they are abandoning you). "Unsafe" is a highly charged word that, unless there is a genuine threat, is often used to make the other person feel like a monster.

2. **The "Need" is a Strategy for Control.** The stated "need for security" is valid, but the unspoken demand is that the only way to meet that need is by controlling the other person's behavior.

3. **The "Request" is a Demand.** There is no room for a "no." If you say no to this "request," you will be accused of not caring about their feelings or their "safety." The conversation is no longer a negotiation;

69

it's a manipulation designed to produce a specific outcome.

This is not a tool for connection; it is a script for coercive control. (We do a full deep dive on this in Chapter 35, but it is critical to be aware of the danger from the start.) A real request leaves room for collaboration; a weaponized one leaves you with an ultimatum. Here is the ultimate litmus test: Does this request create an opportunity for connection, or a demand for compliance?

NO-BULLSHIT TL;DR

- Most difficult conversations fail because they start with blame– a script we all learned. The goal is to connect, not to win.

- **The Script:** "When you…" (State the Observation, not the story).

- **The Feeling:** "I feel…" (State your Feeling, not a judgment).

- **The Need:** "Because I need…" (State your Need, not a strategy).

- **The Request:** "Would you be willing to…?" (Make a specific Request, not a demand).

- Watch out for weaponized language. A true request leaves room for "no"; a demand doesn't.

CHAPTER 9: EMOTIONAL DISTRESS AS A SMOKE ALARM

YOUR BODY'S BUILT-IN BULLSHIT DETECTOR

Let's start by detonating one of the most toxic, damaging, and bullshit myths in the entire landscape of non-monogamy:

If you were really secure / polyamorous / ethical / evolved, you wouldn't feel emotional distress like jealousy, envy, or insecurity.

This is a lie. It is one of the most toxic inherited scripts of the non-monogamy world itself—a weapon used to shame you and a shield used to justify shitty behavior. It is a tool used by others—and your own inner critic—to invalidate perfectly normal human emotions. It is the spiritual bypass at the heart of many dysfunctional "conscious" communities, a tool used to silence dissent and pathologize pain.

Emotional distress isn't a sign that you're doing ENM wrong. It's a sign that you're a human being with a heart, a history, and a nervous system that is wired for attachment. It's a completely predictable—and frankly, logical—response to a perceived threat to a valued connection.

Monogamy promises to protect you from this feeling by putting a locked gate around your relationship. ENM asks you to cultivate a shared garden with an open gate. Emotional distress is not a flaw in the design; it is the smoke alarm blaring inside your own house. It is not a car alarm—a faulty, overly sensitive system that goes off for no reason and should be ignored. Your nervous system is smarter than that. When it screams, there is almost always a fire somewhere, even if it's a small one.

Ignoring it is foolish. Shaming it is counterproductive. Your only useful option is to treat it with the seriousness it demands: walk calmly toward the sound, find the source of the smoke, and figure out what's burning.

DECONSTRUCTING THE DISTRESS: JEALOUSY VS. ENVY VS. INSECURITY

These words are often used interchangeably, but they are not the same thing. Getting specific is the first step toward understanding what the smoke alarm is actually trying to tell you.

Table 9.1: Distinguishing Jealousy, Envy, and Insecurity

Emotion	Definition	Focus	What It Sounds Like
Jealousy	The fear of losing something you have to someone else	A specific person or relationship	"My partner seems so happy with their new date. What if they realize they like them more than me and leave me?"
Envy	The desire for something someone else has that you don't	What someone else has	"My metamour gets to go on a spontaneous weekend trip with our partner. I wish my schedule was that flexible and that I could have that kind of adventurous us time."
Insecurity	A self-focused sense of inadequacy or unworthiness	Yourself	"My partner's other lover is a successful artist who runs marathons. I'm just… me. Why would anyone ever choose to stay with someone so boring when they could be with someone so impressive?"

YOUR REACTION IS THE WHOLE GAME

To make this tangible, let's use an example. Imagine your partner, Your partner, Taylor, is on a date. You agreed they would be home by 11:00 p.m. and would text when leaving. At 10:35 p.m., you get a text: "On my way!" But Taylor doesn't arrive until 12:15 a.m.

Now, let's say you feel that hot spike of jealousy—the pit in your stomach, the clench in your chest, the frantic storytelling in your brain. The cause of that feeling, in itself, is unknown. It's an alarm bell.

What you do next is what defines whether you are practicing ENM or just making things worse. The typical, unhealthy reactions are a masterclass in fanning the flames:

- **The "Cool Girl/Guy" Act (Repression):** You repress the feeling, pretending it doesn't exist to avoid conflict.

- **The Control Freak (Externalization):** You externalize the feeling, making it your partner's problem to solve through new rules or demands.

- **The Punisher (Weaponization):** You weaponize the feeling, ensuring your partner suffers for having a good time without you.

None of these reactions make you less jealous. They just make you, and everyone around you, more miserable. They are understandable, fear-based attempts to find safety using the old tools of the Monogamy Mindset: repression, control, and punishment. They are attempts to outsource your internal emotional work. The alternative is to turn inward first.

THE NO-BULLSHIT DISTRESS EXERCISE: FINDING THE SOURCE OF THE SMOKE

When you feel that familiar spike, don't just react. Investigate. This exercise applies the four-step framework from the previous chapter to help you figure out what your smoke alarm is trying to tell you.

Step 1: The Observation (What Happened?)

First, separate the objective facts from your interpretation.

- **What was the specific trigger?** (e.g., "My partner arrived over an hour after they texted they were on the way home.")

- **What would a video camera have recorded?** (e.g., "Taylor sent a text at 10:35 p.m. and arrived home at 12:15 a.m.

Step 2: The Feeling & The Story (How Do I Feel?)

Next, identify your internal experience without blame.

- **What are the primary emotions I can name?** (e.g., Jealousy, Envy, Insecurity, Fear, Anger, Sadness, Rejection)

- **What is the story I am telling myself about the facts?** Here are some examples of what that might sound like:

- **If the core feeling is Jealousy:** "The story I'm telling myself is that my partner is going to realize they like this new person more than me. This new person is going to replace me, and I'm going to lose my partner." (This is about the fear of losing what you have.)

- **If the core feeling is Envy:** "The story is that my partner is having this amazing, spontaneous, NRE-filled experience. I wish I had that in my life right now. I'm envious of the fun and freedom they're getting to have." (This is about wanting what someone else has.)

- **If the core feeling is Insecurity:** "The story is that they forgot about me and I'm not a priority. It's proof that I'm not interesting or important enough to be remembered." (This is about a negative judgment of yourself.)

Step 3: The Need (What Do I Need?)

Your feelings are messengers pointing to an unmet need.

- **What is the deepest fear this situation is touching?** (e.g., "The fear that I am no longer exciting to them," or "The fear that I am losing them.")

- **This feeling is a signal. What is it signaling that I need right now?** (e.g., "I have a need for reassurance," or "I have a need to feel prioritized and secure.")

Step 4: The Request (What Can I Do?)

Finally, formulate a plan for constructive action, both for yourself and for your relationship.

- **What is one thing I can do for myself right now to self-soothe?** (e.g., "Take a hot bath, call a friend, go for a walk.")

- **What is a clear, collaborative request I can make of my partner later?** (e.g., "When you're running late, could you send me a quick text, so I don't worry?")

- **Do I want to analyze my needs, beliefs, and the script I have been given?** (e.g., Therapy and self-reflection.)

Case Study: Applying the Distress Exercise

Let's see this in action. Liam's partner, Chloe, is on a weekend trip with her other partner, Alex. Liam said he was fine, but Sunday afternoon, he sees an Instagram post: Chloe and

Alex, laughing, holding hands. He feels that hot, sick lurch in his stomach.

His old reaction would be to fire off a passive-aggressive text: "Looks like you're having fun."

Using the tool, he pauses and gets real with himself:

- **Observation:** The trigger is the photo of them holding hands.

- **Feeling:** The feeling is straight-up inadequacy. The story my brain is screaming is, "He's more fun than you. This is proof."

- **Need:** I need to feel like "us" is still solid. I need to feel prioritized and reassured.

- **Request/Action:** My self-soothing action will be to put my phone down and text my buddy to go for a run. The request I will make of Chloe later is for connection and reassurance.

He doesn't dump his anxiety on Chloe while she's away. When she gets home, instead of an accusation, he says, "Welcome back, I missed you. When you have a moment, I'd love to connect. I saw your post and it brought up some insecurity for me, and I could really use some reassurance about us." He's not blaming her for his feeling; he's using the tool to invite her into a conversation about their connection. He is turning his lonely pain into a shared opportunity to strengthen their bond.

THE MYTH OF COMPERSION: IT'S NOT A REQUIREMENT

Compersion—the feeling of vicarious joy you get when your partner is happy with someone else—is real. It's a beautiful, expansive, and worthy aspiration.

But it is not a requirement for Ethical Non-Monogamy. It is not the opposite of jealousy. And for most people, it is almost never spontaneous.

Think of compersion less as a feeling you have and more as a practice you cultivate. It grows slowly, in the soil of trust, security, and good communication. Most importantly, compersion and jealousy can, and often do, coexist in the same moment. You can feel a pang of jealousy in your gut and, simultaneously, a warmth in your heart that your partner is being loved well.

Holding both at once is an advanced skill. Don't shame yourself for not feeling it. The goal isn't to eliminate jealousy in favor of compersion; the goal is to learn the language of all your feelings so you can navigate them with integrity. Once you know what's burning, you can tend to the source of the problem.

PAUSE & CONSIDER

- Recall the last time you felt a spike of jealousy or envy. Mentally walk through the four-step exercise from this chapter:

    1. The Observation: What objectively happened?

2. The Feeling & The Story: What did you feel, and what story did you tell yourself?

3. The Unmet Need: What did that feeling signal that you needed?

4. The Request/Action: What could you have done for yourself in that moment?

- Your jealousy is a messenger, not a monster. The goal is to learn its language.

- What is one thing you can do for yourself the next time that feeling arises, before you ever speak to your partner?

NO-BULLSHIT TL;DR

- Your emotional distress is not a moral failing or a sign you're "bad at poly." It is a functional smoke alarm telling you that a need is not being met.

- The problem isn't the feeling; it's what you do with it. The work is to investigate your feelings with curiosity, not to act them out with blame.

- Use the Distress Exercise to translate your pain into a clear, vulnerable request. This turns a potential conflict into an opportunity for connection.

- Compersion is a wonderful feeling, but it is not a requirement for ethical practice. Learning the language of your jealousy is the real work.

CHAPTER 10: METAMOURS

NAVIGATING THE SHARED PROPERTY LINE

YOUR PARTNER HAS ANOTHER PARTNER.

Take a breath and sit with that sentence. Whether you are the established partner meeting someone new, or the new partner entering an existing dynamic, this reality can be daunting. That other person is not your rival. They are not your replacement. They are not your automatic best friend, your emotional support animal, or your nemesis. They are your **metamour**.

To understand this unique relationship, it helps to use the geometric language of non-monogamy. The most common shape is a **Vee**. In this structure, one person is dating two different people who are not dating each other. That person in the middle is the **hinge**-the person who connects you both, like the point of the letter "V." You and your partner's other partner are at the two top points of the Vee.

You are metamours, connected by your shared partner. You didn't choose them. They didn't choose you. But now your properties are adjacent, connected by a shared interest in the well-being of your mutual partner.

This indirect, and often deeply weird, connection is where the Monogamy Mindset often screams the loudest, telling you that this person is your rival. From the established partner's view, they can feel like a threat. From the new partner's view, they can feel like an intimidating gatekeeper. The work of this chapter is to help everyone involved consciously choose a different script. Getting this dynamic right is a masterclass in emotional maturity. You don't have to be friends. But you do have to be adults.

THE THREE METAMOUR MODELS: A SPECTRUM OF CONNECTION

There is no single correct approach to metamour relationships. Each dynamic typically falls somewhere along a spectrum. The ethical path is finding the model that is genuinely, enthusiastically consensual for all three people involved.

Parallel Polyamory

This model emphasizes independence and privacy. Metamours have little to no direct contact, and communication flows through the hinge partner. For a metamour who values autonomy or is wary of enmeshment, this can feel like a relief. For one who desires a sense of chosen family, it can feel isolating. It relies heavily on the hinge's integrity.

Kitchen Table Polyamory (KTP)

This style aims for a high degree of social comfort among all members of a polycule-the entire network of connected partners. The ideal is that everyone involved could sit down together comfortably at the same kitchen table. For someone seeking a deep, integrated "chosen family," this is the dream. For an introvert or someone with a traumatic family history, it can feel like a performative nightmare. It becomes toxic when forced upon unwilling individuals.

Garden Party Polyamory

This is a moderate middle ground where metamours are cordial at group events but do not form deep personal bonds. This can be a comfortable compromise but risks masking unresolved tensions.

Crucially, your approach can vary. Each relationship should be approached uniquely, based on everyone's comfort and consent.

THE HINGE'S PARADOX: GREAT RESPONSIBILITY, LITTLE CONTROL

Being a hinge is one of the hardest jobs in non-monogamy. You are the central node for communication and emotional management. But let's be brutally clear: You are responsible for your own conduct, but you are *not* responsible for your partners' feelings or for their relationship with each other.

You are a facilitator, not a puppeteer. You cannot force your established partner to be "less insecure," nor can you force your new partner to be "more patient." You cannot control other adults. All the work does not, and should not, belong to you. No one is a perfect hinge all the time; the goal isn't to never make a mistake, but to consistently practice the skills of a good one.

Table 10.1: A Hinge's Diagnostic Checklist

A Skillful Hinge...	An Unskillful Hinge...
Facilitates with Consent: Asks partners what level of interaction they want.	Forces Interaction: Pressures metamours to be friends for their own comfort.
Is an Emotional Firewall: Never vents to one partner about the other.	Triangulates: Creates drama by using one partner as a processor for the other.
Transfers Information Clearly: Relays logistics without emotional spin.	Acts as a "Broken Telephone": Distorts or withholds key information.
Advocates for Both Partners: Ensures both relationships are seen as valid and respected.	Allows Disparagement: Lets one partner dismiss or belittle the other.

A NO-BULLSHIT REALITY CHECK: THE SABOTAGE MIRROR

It's easy to label a partner's resistance as "sabotage." It's a clean narrative that makes them the villain and you the victim. But before you cast them in that role, you have a profound ethical responsibility to look in the mirror and ask the hardest question:

Is the smoke alarm going off because of the new spark, or because your house was already on fire?

Sometimes, a partner's "irrational" jealousy or "controlling" behavior isn't about your new relationship at all. It's a catastrophic, clumsy, but understandable reaction to deep, unaddressed problems in your primary relationship. They aren't trying to sabotage your new connection; they are desperately trying to get you to pay attention to the fact that your shared foundation is crumbling.

Ask yourself, with brutal honesty:

- Have I been using this new relationship as an escape, neglecting core issues at home?

- Is my partner really trying to control me, or are they desperately trying to be heard about a need that has been ignored for months, or years?

- Is this sabotage, or is it a cry for help from a person in a relationship that is failing?

Your new relationship cannot be healthy if it is built on the toxic soil of a failing one.

THE MOST IMPORTANT GUIDELINE: YOU DO NOT HAVE TO BE FRIENDS

This is one of the biggest and most damaging pieces of dogma in ENM. This pressure is often felt most intensely by the new partner, who may feel they have to win the approval of the established one to be considered "valid." Let's be clear: you do not owe deep emotional labor to someone just because you happen to be dating the same person. What you do owe is basic human decency.

And remember, compersion is not the same as liking your metamour. Compersion is joy for your partner's happiness. You can feel deep compersion for your partner while simultaneously not wanting to spend any time with the person who is the source of that joy. Your only obligation is to treat them with the respect you would offer any human being. The rest is a choice, not a requirement.

Table 10.2: A Troubleshooter's Guide to Common Metamour Problems

Issue	What It Might Look Like	What Helps
Forced Friendship	Feeling pressured to bond with a metamour you're not comfortable with.	Normalize Parallel dynamics; affirm that friendship is a gift, not a requirement.
Triangulation	The hinge vents to one partner about the other, letting conflict from one relationship bleed into the other.	Hinge addresses issues within the original dyad or with a therapist; never use a partner as a processor.
Metamour Sabotage	One metamour actively undermines the other relationship out of jealousy, creating drama to test the hinge's loyalty.	Hinge holds a firm boundary. Reinforce that relationships are not a zero-sum game and refuse to be triangulated. The insecure partner must own their emotional work.
Mismatched Expectations	One metamour wants Kitchen Table, the other wants Parallel.	Hinge facilitates a consent-based conversation; compromise based on the person who needs more space.

NO-BULLSHIT TL;DR

- Your metamour is not your rival; they are your neighbor in the relational landscape.

- You get to choose your level of connection. The only right way is the one that is consensual for everyone. Forcing KTP is unethical.

- If you are the hinge, your job is to be a skilled firewall, not a puppeteer. You are responsible for your conduct, not their relationship.

- You do not have to be friends with your metamours. You are only required to treat them with respect.

- Compersion is about celebrating your partner's joy, not about liking your metamour.

CHAPTER 11: THE GARDEN PLAN

BOUNDARIES, RULES, & AGREEMENTS: FENCES, TRELLISES, & BLUEPRINTS

Jealousy hits. Insecurity spikes. The smoke alarm from Chapter 9 is blaring.

In Ethical Non-Monogamy, you are the gardeners of your own connections. To cultivate a thriving relationship garden, you need structure. Three of the most important tools at your disposal are boundaries, rules, and agreements. Think of them like this:

- A **boundary** is a **fence**. It defines what you will and won't allow into your personal space—your property line.

- A **rule** is a **trellis**. It's a temporary structure to support a vulnerable or newly growing part of a relationship while it finds its strength.

- An **agreement** is the **garden plan**. It's the flexible, co-created blueprint that guides how you and your partner will grow together.

Each tool serves a different purpose. Boundaries protect. Rules support. Agreements design. Knowing when and how to use each one is crucial.

Let's be absolutely clear: When that alarm goes off, the first tool most new gardeners reach for isn't a trowel or a watering can. It's a rule. Often wielded like a guardrail, but best thought of as a trellis—a way to give shape and stability to something tender.

Examples of these early-rule moments:

"You cannot sleep over at their place. You must be home by 1:00 AM."

"You can see them and have fun, but no falling in love."

"You have to text me every hour and answer if I call."

This impulse is not only normal; it's a sign of profound care and responsibility. When you're starting out, you have no idea what you are doing. You don't know what these new experiences will feel like, and you don't yet have the shared language or trust to build flexible agreements. A rule is a necessary trellis. It's a clear, simple structure you build together to hold the relationship safely while it learns to grow. Anyone who tells you that you shouldn't need rules to feel safe is either a fool or a predator, asking you to walk into a minefield blindfolded and call it freedom.

Rules are not signs of failure or weakness. They are trellises—temporary supports for relationships still growing toward the light. The danger isn't in having them. The danger is in forgetting to revisit them, in letting trellises become cages.

A WORD OF WARNING: BEWARE THE IDEOLOGUE

As you build your first trellises, you will almost certainly encounter someone who will judge your process. They will say things that sound evolved, like:

"If you really trust each other, you shouldn't need rules."

"The point is to be free. You're just building a new cage for yourselves."

This person is not your guru. They are offering you dogma, not wisdom, and that can be poison to a relationship in a fragile state. The agreements you and your partner make in private to ensure you both feel safe are your business. Period. Being told you are "doing it wrong" for needing a rule is like being shamed for putting up a fence to protect a new garden from deer. Ignore them. Your first responsibility is to the well-being of your own garden, not to someone else's idea of what a "perfect" garden should look like.

A WORD ON A TOXIC MYTH

Let's call out a toxic myth you'll encounter in some ENM spaces: the idea that "radical autonomy" means you should never do anything for a partner that isn't 100% for your own pleasure. This philosophy of "your journey is all that matters" is not freedom; its selfishness wearing a progressive hat.

A relationship is a team sport. Of course, your partner's feelings should be a factor in your decisions. Of course, there will be give and take. This isn't being controlled or shamed; it's called being a decent, loving partner. Healthy interdependence isn't about sacrificing your autonomy; it's about consciously choosing to factor your partner's well-being into your decisions, and trusting that they will do the same for you. The work of this chapter is not to erase that interdependence but to make it conscious and consensual.

THE GARDENER'S TOOLKIT: FENCES, TRELLISES, & GARDEN PLANS

1. The Fence (Your Boundary)

A boundary is a fence you build to protect your own property. It's a statement about *your* actions, not your partner's. It's the instruction manual for how another person can be close to you without causing harm.

Let's destigmatize this immediately. Boundaries are not punitive walls. They are not a sign that you are damaged or demanding. A healthy boundary is simply the instruction manual for how another person can be close to you without causing harm. A person who respects you will welcome this clarity; a person who pushes against your boundaries is showing you they are not safe.

The difference between a boundary and a controlling rule is simple:

- A **rule** says: "You can't yell in my garden." (This controls their behavior).

- A **boundary** says: "If you start yelling in my garden, I will go back inside my house." (This controls your behavior).

  Example of a boundary (the fence): Imagine your partner keeps pressing you for sexual details you've said you don't want to share. A boundary is not demanding they stop; it's defining what you will do: "I am not willing to share these kinds of details. If you continue to ask, I will end the conversation."

2. The Trellis (A Rule)

A rule is a temporary trellis you install to support a young or struggling relationship until it's strong enough to stand on its own. It is a rigid structure designed to manage risk and provide security.

- **A Rule for Others:** A directive you ask a partner to follow to help you feel safe. Example: "For the next three months, can we have a rule that we don't bring new partners to our home?"

- **A Rule for Yourself:** A conscious act of self-discipline. Example: "My personal rule is that I will not check my metamour's social media for the next month because I know it triggers my insecurity."

The danger is when a trellis is never removed. It becomes a permanent cage that chokes the very connection it was meant to support. The key difference between a healthy rule and a toxic one is its intentionality and a built-in plan for its own evolution.

3. The Garden Plan (Your Agreements)

An agreement is the collaborative garden plan you and your partner design together. It's what healthy, temporary rules evolve into once trust is established. Agreements are flexible, mutually beneficial understandings built on trust, not fear.

Example of a foundational agreement: "We agree to let each other know when we have a date scheduled, including the person's name and general location for safety. We also agree to always update each other on our safer sex status. This plan feels good to both of us."

Example of an advanced agreement (navigating shared crushes): "Okay, we both agree Sarah is amazing. I'm feeling a really strong pull to explore that connection first. Would you be willing to take a step back for a month to give me that space? We can check in afterward and see how everyone feels." This isn't a demand; it's a collaborative request built on deep trust and a shared desire for each other's happiness.

- **The Emergency Override:** Life is unpredictable. A significant event—a health diagnosis, a family crisis—is a valid reason to call an "emergency meeting" to re-evaluate a rule.

- **The Early Graduation Option:** Sometimes, you learn faster than you thought. It's okay to mutually agree that a rule has served its purpose and let it go. This is a testament to its success.

A trellis that is thoughtfully designed, mutually agreed upon, and has a clear plan for its own evolution is not a cage. It is an act of profound, collaborative care—two people agreeing to build a railing so they can safely admire the view from a scary cliff, together.

Table 11.1: Distinguishing Boundaries, Rules, and Agreements

Feature	Boundary (Your Fence)	Rule (A Temporary Trellis)	Agreement (The Garden Plan)
Core Question	"What must I do to keep myself safe?"	"What must you do (temporarily) so I can feel safe?"	"What will we do together to build trust?"
Who It Controls	Yourself. It governs your own actions and choices.	Others. It is a request to limit a partner's behavior.	The Team. It is a co-created plan that governs your shared dynamic.
The Litmus Test	Sounds like: "If you do X, I will…"	Sounds like: "To feel safe, I need you to not do X."	Sounds like: "We agree to do X together."
Source	Your own values and needs.	A responsible need for structure in the face of inexperience. It can also be born from fear.	Mutual trust and a shared desire for a sustainable connection.
Healthiest Use	To protect your non-negotiables with integrity.	As temporary scaffolding while trust and skills are being built.	As the flexible, living blueprint for your relationship.
When It Becomes Toxic	When a "boundary" is actually a disguised rule to control others.	When it is permanent, unilateral, and used as a cage to manage anxiety.	When it's created under duress or is not truly co-created by all parties.

NO-BULLSHIT TL;DR

- Know your tools. Boundaries are your fence (protecting you), rules are a temporary trellis (supporting a new growth), and agreements are the living garden plan you design together.

- Rules are useful training wheels, but they become toxic cages when they are permanent, unilateral, and born from the fear of the Monogamy Mindset.

- The goal is always to evolve temporary, fear-based rules into flexible, trust-based agreements.

- Healthy gardens require regular tending. Your agreements are living documents that must be revisited and nurtured to thrive.

CHAPTER 12: THE DAILY TENDING

WEEDS, WATER & WEATHER

You've done the hard work. You've sat down with your partner(s), had the vulnerable conversations, and co-designed a beautiful Garden Plan. The initial agreements are in place. The fences are clear. The first seeds of trust have been planted.

So, now you can just relax and let it grow, right?

This is the most common—and most dangerous—misconception in all of relationships, monogamous or not. The belief that a relationship, once established, can be put on autopilot is the silent killer of connection. A garden that is not tended will not flourish. It will be overrun by weeds, starved of water, and baked by the sun until it is a dry, barren plot.

WHAT KIND OF GARDEN ARE YOU TENDING?

Before we talk about tools, let's be honest about what we're working with. The "Shared Garden" is a flexible metaphor because not all relationships are the same. Understanding the specific type of garden you're cultivating with each person is critical to knowing what kind of care it requires.

A deeply romantic, cohabitating partnership is a sprawling shared vegetable garden. It's deeply integrated into your daily life and requires constant attention: regular watering (quality time), pest control (conflict resolution), and a shared planting schedule (managing calendars and life goals).

A casual, fun, once-a-month connection might be a single, beautiful potted plant on the porch. It needs weekly watering (a conversation), fertilizer (flirty texts or pictures), and a check-in every six months to see if it's happy in its current pot or needs more space to grow and evolve. This plant brings you joy, but it doesn't require the same complex care as a vegetable garden.

If you're practicing solo polyamory, you might be tending to several distinct, separate gardens that don't overlap. The primary work isn't co-weeding one plot; it's managing your own time and energy to travel between them, ensuring each one gets the unique attention it needs to thrive on its own terms.

The No-Bullshit Reality: Larger, more entangled gardens require more work. This isn't a moral judgment. A sprawling garden isn't "better" than a potted plant; it's just more complex. The goal is to be honest about the kind of relationship you are actually cultivating with someone so you can bring the right amount of water and tools to the job. Asking someone who only signed up to care for a potted plant to help you till a five-acre farm is a recipe for burnout and resentment.

THE BULLSHIT OF THE PERFECT, WEED-FREE GARDEN

Here's the no-bullshit truth about gardens and relationships: weeds are going to grow. There is no stopping them. They are a natural and inevitable part of any living ecosystem. Small resentments, unspoken discomforts, and tiny misalignments will always sprout.

The goal of a healthy relationship is not to have a perfectly manicured, weed-free garden. That is a performance, not a partnership. Beware the person who shames you for having weeds in your garden. Every relationship has them. Some people are just better at hiding them or only pulling the ones that are visible from the street.

The real work is not to prevent all problems, but to create a sustainable practice of tending to them. Sometimes you'll pull them out right away. Sometimes you won't have the energy, and that's okay. A small weed might be harder to remove later, but as long as it isn't strangling the core of the plant, you can tend to it when you have the capacity. Ethical practice demands moving from a "set-it-and-forget-it" mindset to one of "check-in-and-gently-weed." This is the foundation of a "Good Enough" Garden—one that is resilient, alive, and real.

THE MAINTENANCE SCHEDULE: THE GARDEN WALKTHROUGH

Start by noticing willingness.

"Thanks for doing this with me. If today isn't workable, can we pick a time we both can handle?" If they won't look together, that's the first issue: you can't tend what you won't look at. Name the impasse without shaming—"It's hard to work on this if we don't look together"—and decide how you'll handle the refusal:

- **Shorten the walk:** Two-minute scan, one choice, one action. That's all.

- **Time-box everything:** Set a timer and stop when it dings. Relief beats resentment.

- **Trade agency:** "You pick the focus today; I'll pick next time."

If willingness is **zero** over time, the problem isn't logistics; it's consent to maintenance. Treat that as the topic and consider outside help.

Match scope to capacity.

Let the length and depth fit the focus, energy, and ability of whoever has the least of those today. Push for less, not more. Ten honest minutes that end in one real action beat ninety minutes of forced "processing." If one of you is at a 3/10, aim for a 3/10-sized walkthrough. "I've got a heavy week and early mornings; I have about fifteen minutes in me. Let's keep the scope small."

Look together at what's here.

Walk the garden side by side. Name what's grown strong or beautiful, what's been ignored, and what needs a simple touch-up. Stay descriptive; avoid verdicts. You are not fixing the whole garden at once. Think headlines:

- *What's working:* the shared calendar helped; we planned a date night.

- *What's stressed:* money talks keep slipping; finding a therapist; feelings about last Saturday.

- *Needs a touch-up:* bedtime logistics when the kids switch houses.

Choose only what you both agree to.

From the real limits in front of you (work, family, health, money, attention), pick the few items you can realistically move now. "Money, therapy, or feelings—*which one* do we both actually want to look at this week?"

Agreement matters more than ambition. If you can't both say "yes," it's not a focus; let it wait until the next walkthrough. The goal is direction, not forced harmony.

Make it actionable.

Translate the choice into concrete moves: **who** will do **what**, by **when**, and **how you'll both know** it happened. Put actions where you'll see them (calendar, shared note, whiteboard). If it isn't written and dated, it's a wish.

One-sentence commitment template (to avoid vague promises): "I will [specific action] on [date/time] so that [shared purpose]. We'll know it happened because [evidence/where it lives]."

Examples

- "I'll make a one-page outline for our money chat (balances, upcoming bills, one tweak) and share it tonight. Let's try it Wednesday at 6:30 p.m. I'll put it on our shared calendar so it's visible and we can check it off."

- "I'll email the therapist shortlist by Tuesday 7 p.m. so we can pick together; the list will be in our shared Notes."

Look forward together.

Confirm the actions and put one or two future plans you both want on the calendar—something concrete to look forward to. *"Let's put the park picnic on the 12th."* Plan quick check-ins over time to see what's working and what still needs a touch-up. This can be as light as: "Next Sunday we'll check in for five minutes."

Adapting to different contexts

- **Low energy / mental health days:** Say your capacity up front. Keep it brief: name one thing going well, one thing that's hard, and one small step you can actually take— then stop.

- **Multiple partners / households:** Duplicate the walkthrough per relationship; don't try to merge every garden into one walk.

- **Neurodivergent brains:** Visuals may help. Use a whiteboard or color-coded checklist; keep the walkthrough predictable (same day/time, same two opening questions).

THE ART OF THE SMALL APOLOGY: PULLING WEEDS QUICKLY

Tending isn't just about scheduled check-ins; it's also about how you handle small, everyday missteps. Not every broken agreement is a catastrophic rupture that requires the crisis protocol in the next chapter. Sometimes, you're just clumsy. You forget to text. You say something insensitive. You mismanage your time.

These are the most common kind of weeds in any garden. They aren't a sign of a crisis; they are just the normal friction of life. But if you let them sit, they foster resentment. The key is to pull them out quickly and cleanly. A small, sincere apology is the best tool for this.

WHEN MAINTENANCE ISN'T ENOUGH

You can do everything right—you can water diligently, weed constantly, and check the soil every week—and a storm can still come and flatten your garden. The tools discussed here are designed to help manage the common aspects of a relationship. They are designed to handle sun, shade, and gentle rain.

But sometimes, what you thought was a weed is actually an invasive species poisoning the soil. A hailstorm of betrayal hits without warning, and the damage isn't minor; it's a deep, structural rupture.

When that happens, the tools of routine maintenance are not enough. You need an emergency protocol. You need triage. And that is what we will cover next.

NO-BULLSHIT TL;DR

- There is no such thing as a perfect, weed-free relationship. Weeds (resentments, misalignments) are normal. The goal is a resilient "Good Enough" Garden, not a flawless one.

- The Garden Walkthrough is a powerful, structured tool for the gentle, regular weeding that keeps a relationship healthy.

- Pull the small weeds quickly. A simple, sincere apology for a minor misstep prevents it from growing into a major resentment.

- This routine care keeps your relationship resilient, but it can't prevent every crisis.

CHAPTER 13: WHEN AGREEMENTS ARE BROKEN

A TRIAGE PROTOCOL FOR RELATIONAL RUPTURES

No matter how perfect your garden plan or how loving your intentions, things will break. Because we are all imperfect people, acting from a lifetime of unexamined scripts, there will be misunderstandings, hurt feelings, and accidental missteps. These are the normal frictions of tending a garden with another person.

But sometimes, something bigger happens. A line is crossed. A core agreement is violated. This is a **rupture**—a significant break in the trust or safety of your shared garden. It might be a trampled flower from an accidental lapse, or it might be a catastrophic act of sabotage that poisons the soil and threatens the entire plot.

This moment doesn't automatically mean your relationship is doomed. It doesn't mean ENM is a failed experiment. But it does mean you've reached a critical threshold that demands more than a simple "I'm sorry." How you navigate the rupture will define the character of your relationship more than any happy moment ever could. It requires unflinching honesty, profound humility, and a series of very hard decisions. This is the moment where the "ethical" part of ENM is truly put to the test.

Ruptures happen in all relationships; a healthy one is not a relationship with no ruptures, but one with a reliable process for repair. This is the moment a catastrophic storm has hit your garden, and the work shifts from routine tending to emergency triage.

ASSESSING THE DAMAGE: A SPECTRUM OF RUPTURE

Not all violations are created equal. When you are reeling from a betrayal, it's natural to lump every violation together under the single, painful banner of "cheating." It can feel impossible to find the energy for nuance when you are just trying to cope. But to navigate the aftermath ethically, your first job is to gently pause, take a breath, and assess the actual severity of the damage so you can match your response to the level of harm. It's helpful to think of these breaches on a spectrum, like physical injuries: you don't treat a paper cut and a compound fracture the same way.

Table 13.1: A Spectrum of Relational Rupture

Level	Description	Examples	Recommended Response
1	Minor Friction: Accidental missteps or misunderstandings	Forgetting to share a calendar update; clumsy wording that causes hurt	Gentle check-in, clarification, and small repair conversations
2	Significant Breach: A core agreement is broken, but not with malicious intent	Breaking safer sex agreements; hiding a date; failing to disclose something important	Space, pause, formal apology, clear plan for repair, and possible relationship re-negotiation
3	Major Rupture: A profound betrayal or pattern of harm	Repeated deception; manipulative behavior; emotional gaslighting	Full pause, external support (e.g., therapist), and potential relationship overhaul or ending

The goal of this initial period is not to solve the problem; it is to stop doing more damage

If you are the one who was hurt

- **Prioritize Your Safety.** Your only job right now is to get safe. That's it. If your body is telling you to leave the house, walk out the door. If your gut is screaming for you to call a friend, pick up the phone. This is not a moment for negotiation; it is a moment for action. Whatever safety looks like, go there now.

- **Resist The Urge To Understand.** You will want answers. You will want to know why. That can come later. Right now, demanding an explanation while you are both in shock will likely lead to a defensive, unproductive fight that causes more damage.

- **State Your Need For A Pause.** You are in charge of the timeline. A powerful script is: "I have just learned something that has broken my trust. I am in shock, and I am hurting. I cannot have a productive conversation right now. I need space. We will talk about this [tomorrow / in two days / after my therapy appointment]."

- **Do Not Make Any Major Decisions.** Don't decide to break up. Don't decide to forgive. Don't decide anything. Your only decision right now is to create a safe container for your own emotional processing.

If you are the one who broke the agreement

- **Stop Talking. Start Listening.** Your impulse will be to explain, justify, and defend yourself to mitigate your own shame. Your intent does not matter right now. Their impact does.

- **Give A Clean, Simple Acknowledgment.** No excuses. Just the facts. "Yes, it is true. I broke our agreement. I understand that this is devastating."

- **Honor Their Need For Space.** If they ask for a pause, you must grant it without argument or guilt. Pushing to "talk it out now" is a selfish act designed to soothe your anxiety, not to help them.

- **Make No Demands.** You do not get to ask for forgiveness, understanding, or even a hug. You have forfeited your right to be centered. Your job is to be humble, patient, and to wait.

THE ANATOMY OF A REAL APOLOGY (WHEN YOU'RE BOTH READY)

Accountability is not just saying, "I'm sorry." After the initial crisis has passed and both parties are regulated enough to talk, the person who caused the harm must offer a real apology. It is the non-negotiable first step toward any potential repair. A bad apology—"I'm sorry I hurt you, but…" —is just an excuse in disguise; the "but" negates everything that came before it. A real apology is a multi-step process of taking ownership.

A real apology must include:

- **A Clear Statement of the Harmful Action.** No weasel words. "I broke our fluid-bonding agreement." "I lied to you about my relationship with Sarah."

- **A Sincere Acknowledgment of the Impact.** "I know that by doing so, I betrayed your trust, put your physical health at risk, and made you question the reality of our relationship. I understand that this is devastating."

- **An Expression of Genuine Remorse.** "I am deeply sorry for the pain, fear, and chaos I have caused you." (This is not "I'm sorry you feel that way.")

- **A Statement of What You Will Do Differently (Your Repair Plan).** "I am scheduling a full STI panel tomorrow. I am going to find a therapist to understand why I made such a reckless choice. I commit to not engaging in any sexual activity with anyone until we have a clear and safe path forward."

- **A Request for What They Need for Repair.** "I know I don't get to decide what happens next. I am open to hearing what you might need from me to even begin to feel safe again, even if I can't promise I can provide it."

- **An Acceptance That Repair Is Not Guaranteed.** "I understand that even if I do all this work, you may still decide that you cannot continue this relationship. I will respect that decision without pressure or guilt. Your healing and safety are what matter most."

This conversation is not the end of the process. It is the formal beginning of the next, much longer one: the hard work of rebuilding.

NO-BULLSHIT TL;DR

- Not all broken agreements are equal. Differentiate between a minor friction, a significant breach, and a major rupture to guide your response.

- In the first 24 hours after a major breach, the only goal is triage: stop doing more damage. Do not try to solve the problem while in shock.

- The hurt person's job is to seek safety. The person who caused harm's job is to be humble, listen, and give space.

- A real apology isn't just words; it's a multi-step process of accountability that includes a concrete plan for changed behavior. This is the first step on the long road to repair.

PART 3: THE DEEP DIVES

CHAPTER 14: POLYAMORY

NAVIGATING MULTIPLE DEEP, EMOTIONAL CONNECTIONS

This is the heavyweight champion of the ENM world—the term that carries the most cultural baggage, the most utopian ideals, and often, the most potential for spectacular, heartbreaking failure. Just as monogamy has its fairytale script of "The One," polyamory has its own romanticized script of a beautiful, harmonious web of enlightened lovers. It's a beautiful theory.

If you've been practicing it for years, you know the reality is far messier. It can feel less like a utopian web and more like a tangle of tripwires, a minefield of miscommunication, a full-time job in emotional labor, and the unique circle of hell that is trying to sync three people's Google Calendars just to find a Tuesday evening for a date.

Case Study: A Vee-Style Polycule

Maria is dating both Sam and Chloe. Last week, Sam felt neglected because Maria spent three nights with Chloe, who was going through a family emergency. Instead of telling Maria, Sam vented to his best friend, who advised him to demand "equal time." This led to a tense, rights-based conversation with Maria, who felt torn and misunderstood.

A more skillful approach would have been for Sam to use the Unf*ckable Conversation Framework from Chapter 8: "When you spent three nights with Chloe last week, I felt lonely and insecure. I have a need to feel like we're still solid and that I'm a priority for you. Would you be willing to schedule a dedicated date night for just us this week?" Theoretical ideals of fairness can become messy tripwires without direct, vulnerable communication.

The Path Forward: The work for Sam is not to blame Maria for his feelings, but to own his need for connection and make a vulnerable request. The work for Maria is to hear that request with compassion, even while managing her own crisis. This isn't about scorekeeping ("equal time"); it's about the ongoing, messy work of tending to multiple connections with care.

WHAT POLYAMORY IS (AND ISN'T)

At its core, **polyamory** (from the Greek *poly* for "many" and the Latin *amor* for "love") means having, or being open to having, more than one romantic, emotionally intimate relationship at a time—with the full knowledge and informed consent of everyone involved.

But that definition is just the skeleton. The lived experience is the flesh and blood. Polyamory is not just a different set of rules; it's a different way of relating, requiring a whole new suite of skills.

Polyamory is NOT:

- **A fancy word for swinging or a casual open relationship.** The defining characteristic of polyamory is the acceptance, and often the encouragement, of ongoing emotional intimacy and romantic connection with multiple people. It's about hearts, not just genitals. If your agreements include a "no feelings" rule, you are not practicing polyamory.

- **A cure for your internal problems.** While a polyamorous life can be rich with connection, it can also be profoundly lonely. There's a unique, gut-wrenching loneliness in feeling insecure while your partner is out on a date with someone they're falling for. If you are lonely within yourself, adding more people will only make you feel lonelier in more crowded rooms.

- **A fix for a broken partnership.** This cannot be stressed enough. Using polyamory to salvage a failing relationship is like trying to fix a sinking ship by drilling more holes in the hull. Polyamory is a powerful magnifier; it will not fix what is already broken. It will amplify existing cracks until they shatter.

- **The opposite of commitment.** This is a fundamental misunderstanding. Polyamorous people often form deeply committed, lifelong partnerships. They simply don't believe that commitment must equal sexual or romantic exclusivity. The commitment is to the person and the well-being of the relationship, not to a specific structure of ownership.

THE GEOMETRY OF LOVE: A FEW KEY TERMS

To discuss these complex dynamics, the community has developed a shared vocabulary to describe its common shapes. The entire network of all significant connections is known as a **polycule**. Within that network, the most common structure is a **Vee**, where one person, the **hinge**, is romantically involved with two other people who are not dating each other. Those two people are **metamours** to one another.

Less common is a **triad** (or **throuple**), where all three people are in a direct relationship with each other. A polycule might also include an **anchor partner**, who provides a deep sense of stability, or a **comet**, a significant partner you see infrequently due to distance. Knowing your own limits and when you are **polysaturated**—at your full capacity for maintaining healthy relationships—is a critical skill.

A DEEP DIVE INTO POLYAMOROUS STRUCTURES: THE HIERARCHY DEBATE

One of the most contentious topics in polyamory is **hierarchy**—the practice of ranking relationships by priority or importance. Broadly, polyamorous relationships can be structured in a few key ways.

Descriptive Hierarchy This is an honest description of existing life entanglements, like a marriage or shared children. It sounds like: "I'm married with kids, so I can't offer cohabitation." It acknowledges reality without imposing control on other partners.

Table 14.1: A Hierarchy Litmus Test: Descriptive vs. Prescriptive

Feature	Descriptive Hierarchy (Ethical)	Prescriptive Hierarchy (Unethical)
Core Purpose	To honestly describe existing life entanglements (e.g., kids, mortgage, marriage).	To prescribe rules that control other partners' feelings and behaviors to protect the primary dyad.
The Focus	On stating your own limitations and capacity.	On limiting your partner's autonomy and connections.
What It Sounds Like	"Because I am married, I cannot offer you cohabitation or children."	"Because we are married, you cannot fall in love with my partner or see them on holidays."
Impact on Other Partners	They feel respected and informed about the real-world constraints from the start.	They are treated as "less than," disposable, and a potential threat to be managed.
The Veto Question	A veto is incompatible. You don't get to fire your partner's other partners.	A veto is often a central feature—a "panic button" to enforce the power imbalance.
The No-Bullshit Verdict	This is an act of honesty.	This is an act of control.

Prescriptive Hierarchy This is an unethical structure that uses rules not just to describe reality, but to enforce a power imbalance and control other partners. It fundamentally treats some partners as "less than" others. It sounds like: "We have a rule that you can't come to Thanksgiving because you're my secondary partner." This is where a **veto**—the power for one partner to unilaterally end another's relationship—is often wielded as a tool of control, making the secondary partner disposable.

Non-Hierarchical Polyamory This approach values all relationships organically without a formal ranking, allowing each connection to find its own level. It sounds like: "Let's see what this connection becomes on its own terms." In this model, a veto is considered fundamentally incompatible with its philosophy of autonomy.

Case Study: The Squeaky Hinge

Consider a common hinge failure. Alex is on the phone with their partner, Ben, after a tense conversation with their other partner, Sarah.

- **A dysfunctional response (dumping and triangulating):** Alex sighs, "Ugh, Sarah's being so anxious about the schedule again. I don't get why she can't just be chill about things, you know? Like you are." In this version, Alex makes Ben an accomplice in judging Sarah, poisoning the well between his two partners.

- **An ethical response (seeking support without triangulating):** Alex says, "I had a really difficult conversation with Sarah about scheduling, and I'm feeling stressed and overwhelmed. Could I just get a hug?" Here, Alex owns their emotional state and asks for comfort without making Sarah the villain.

  The No-Bullshit Difference: The ethical hinge seeks support from one partner without making the other partner the problem. They own their feelings and ask for co-regulation, keeping the conflict contained within the relationship where it belongs.

NO-BULLSHIT TL;DR

- Polyamory is defined by its focus on multiple, emotionally intimate relationships. If your agreements forbid feelings, it's not polyamory.

- Hierarchy is ethical when it describes your reality (like marriage or kids), but unethical when it prescribes rules to control others' feelings or relationships.

- The hinge partner's integrity is the load-bearing wall of the entire structure. Triangulation and conflict avoidance will cause a collapse.

- Forcing friendship with metamours (KTP) is a common form of dogma. Respect is required; friendship is a gift.

- Polyamory is a powerful magnifier. It will not fix a broken relationship; it will amplify the cracks until they shatter.

CHAPTER 15: SWINGING

THE SOCIAL SIDE OF SEXUAL FREEDOM

If polyamory is the heavyweight champion of emotional entanglement, then swinging is the heavyweight champion of social and sexual exploration. Let's be clear: swinging isn't a fringe activity or a "lite" version of non-monogamy. For many, it is the original, foundational form of ENM, with a vibrant, global community often referred to as "The Lifestyle."

The core philosophy here is different from polyamory, but it is no less valid. The goal is not necessarily to build new, deep romantic relationships. Instead, swinging is often a couple-centric practice. The primary intent is to explore sexuality with others as a team, with the explicit goal of bringing energy, excitement, and a deeper bond back into the primary relationship.

You're not necessarily looking for more romantic partners. You're a couple, you love each other, and you want to stay together. Your foundation is strong, but you're also curious. You want to meet new, interesting people and explore your sexuality together, in a way that feels exciting and new.

WHAT SWINGING IS (AND ISN'T)

Swinging is a form of Ethical Non-Monogamy that centers on a couple's shared adventure into social and sexual exploration. The goal isn't to find new romantic partners; it's to have recreational sex together, with the explicit intent of bringing that energy and excitement back to the primary relationship.

Let's be brutally clear: this is a difference in goals, not in moral high ground. Polyamory isn't more "evolved" than swinging. They are different tools for different jobs. The only ethical failure is showing up with a hammer when you secretly want a screwdriver, lying to your partners about your intentions, or bullying your partner into a renovation project they never wanted.

The Emotional Realities: It's Not "Simpler," It's Just Different

A common misconception is that a focus on sex over romantic connection is "simpler" or "less messy." This is a dangerous and naive illusion. The emotional terrain is just different, not easier. And these challenges are not unique to people who call themselves swingers. Any polyamorous person who explores casual connections or attends play parties will encounter this same landscape. The challenges are focused more on ego, insecurity, and performance in a highly charged sexual environment.

The Partnership Test: Navigating Mismatched Desire

Here's the fantasy: you and your partner will walk into a party, spot another couple, and lightning will strike twice. You'll be intensely attracted to one of them, and your partner will be just as attracted to the other. It's a perfect, symmetrical swap.

Now, here's the no-bullshit reality: **That almost never happens.**

Far more often, you'll find a couple where you're intensely attracted to one person, and your partner feels… lukewarm about the other. This predictable mismatch of desire is not a problem to be solved; it is the fundamental test of your partnership. How you navigate it reveals everything about your dynamic—whether you are a truly collaborative team or a partnership built on subtle (or not-so-subtle) pressure.

- **A dysfunctional dynamic (subtle pressure):** One partner's lack of enthusiasm is treated as an obstacle to the other's fun, creating a quiet accusation: Your feelings are a problem I need you to solve so I can get what I want.

- **A healthy partnership (teamwork):** One partner's lack of enthusiasm is treated as valid information. Their comfort is held as the highest priority. This creates a sense of safety, which often allows the hesitant partner to engage not as a concession but as a genuine act of partnership.

Red Flags: Vetting Individuals and Couples

- **The Hidden Spouse:** A person claims their partner is "totally cool with this," but you never meet or speak to this partner.

Do not proceed. You may be unknowingly participating in cheating.

- **The Feigned Interest:** One person feigns interest in you just to get access to your partner. Someone with integrity will be honest about their primary attraction while still treating you with respect.

- **The Dismissal:** A couple makes it clear they are only interested in one of you and that the other is an inconvenient obstacle. This is objectification.

Common psychological and emotional challenges include:

- **Insecurity and Performance Anxiety:** Watching your partner be incredibly turned on by someone else can be a gut punch to the ego.

- **Pacing Mismatch:** One partner is a social butterfly while the other is an overwhelmed wallflower. Pushing the hesitant partner is a fast track to resentment.

- **The Bait-and-Switch:** One partner claims to be okay, participates enthusiastically, and then punishes their partner with a week of emotional shutdown.

- **Lack of Aftercare:** This is one of the biggest mistakes people make in any form of casual play. After an intense night, partners must reconnect. Aftercare—cuddling, reassurance, talking—is mandatory.

- **Catching Feelings (The Polyamory-Swinging Bridge):** This is one of the most predictable and destabilizing challenges. You agree to a dynamic that is "just sex," but then you or your partner develop a deep, romantic, and lasting connection with a play partner. Sex is an intimate act, and pretending we can build a perfect firewall against emotion is naive. This isn't a sign of failure, but it is a moment of crisis that demands radical honesty. If one person has "crossed the bridge" into polyamory while the other wants to remain in swinging, the original agreement is broken and must be renegotiated from scratch.

VETTING THE SPACE: PROBLEMATIC POLITICS IN THE ENM SCENE

Be aware that many sex-focused social spaces—whether they call themselves swinger clubs, play parties, or kink dungeons—can be minefields of unexamined privilege. While these issues can appear anywhere, they are often amplified in environments where bodies are on display. This can look like:

- **Lookism and Fatphobia:** Spaces often cater to conventionally attractive, able-bodied couples.

- **Problematic Pricing:** Charging single men exorbitant fees while letting single women in for free commodifies women's presence.

- **Biphobia and Double Standards:** The scene often hypersexualizes bisexual women while stigmatizing bisexual men. The infamous one penis policy (OPP), where a man allows his female partner to play only with other women, is a classic example of this hetero-patriarchal control.

- **Racial Fetishization:** The term "bull," for example, is often used to seek out Black men to fulfill a specific racialized sexual fantasy, which is a form of objectification.

A TOUR OF SWINGING STYLES & TERMS

Table 15.1: Common Swinging Terminology and Dynamics

Term	Definition	Context or Note
Soft Swap	Engaging in sexual activities with others that exclude penetrative sex	Often used as a way for couples to explore gradually
Full Swap	Engaging in penetrative sex with others outside the primary couple	Considered "all in" by many in the lifestyle
Same-Room Play	Both partners engage with others in the same physical space	Encourages shared experience; helps some feel more connected
Separate-Room Play	Partners play with others in different spaces	Requires high levels of trust and communication
Unicorn	A (usually bisexual) woman willing to date or play with a couple.	Often fetishized or objectified; ethical unicorn hunting requires treating the person as a full partner, not an accessory.
Hotwife	A woman in a committed relationship who plays with others, often with her partner's encouragement.	Can be an empowering or performative role depending on consent dynamics. The dynamic is centered on her pleasure and agency.
Bull	A man who has sex with a partnered woman in a "hotwife" dynamic, often with the partner present or with their full encouragement.	Be cautious: the term is often racially fetishized (specifically seeking Black men). Use with awareness and consent.

THE NO-BULLSHIT REALITY: WHEN THE LINES BLUR

So far, we've drawn a hard, clear line between polyamory (multiple emotional relationships) and swinging (recreational sex). We did that for a reason: understanding the difference in core intent is the most critical first step in navigating ENM. If you can't be honest with yourself and your partners about whether you're seeking hearts or just bodies, you're heading for disaster.

But the real world is often messier than a textbook definition. Can a person or a couple be both polyamorous and swingers? Yes.

Many people in the ENM community practice a hybrid style. For example:

- **The "Polyswinger":** This might be a polyamorous couple who has deep, committed, ongoing relationships with other people, but who also enjoys attending swinger parties for more casual, recreational sexual encounters that don't involve deep emotional entanglement.

- **Swingers Who Evolve:** This might be a couple who identifies as swingers for years, but then develops a deep, romantic, and lasting connection with another couple or individual they met at a club, and their dynamic evolves into polyamory.

The label you use is far less important than the reality you live. The goal is not to fit perfectly into a box called "polyamory" or "swinging." The goal is to have the self-awareness to know what you're seeking in any given connection, and the integrity to communicate that honestly to everyone involved. The most ethical practice is to be clear about your intentions, moment by moment, person by person.

NO-BULLSHIT TL;DR

- Swinging is about a couple's shared adventure, not finding new partners. It's a different toolkit than polyamory—neither is more "evolved."

- The emotional challenges of sex-focused non-monogamy—like performance anxiety and navigating mismatched desire—are intense and not "simpler" than polyamory's challenges.

- This advice applies to anyone in ENM who engages in casual or group play. The need for clear agreements, honest debriefs, and robust aftercare is universal.

- Be aware of problematic politics in sex-focused spaces. Vet your venues and partners, and prioritize your safety and values.

CHAPTER 16: OPEN RELATIONSHIPS

NAVIGATING CUSTOM AGREEMENTS & RENOVATIONS

Let's talk about "open relationship"—one of the most overused, under-defined, and potentially explosive phrases in the non-monogamy world. It sounds progressive. Chill. Casual.

But here's the problem with that seductive ambiguity: "We're open" often means wildly different things to each partner. One person hears "open" and thinks, "Great, we can have casual sex." The other hears "open" and thinks, "Finally, I can explore that romantic connection." When those two interpretations collide without a clarifying conversation, the result isn't freedom; it's a chaotic mess.

An "open relationship" isn't a pre-set model; it is a custom renovation project for an existing garden. To navigate it successfully, you must move beyond vague labels and create a brutally specific, co-created blueprint. This is where the tools from Chapter 11 ("The Garden Plan") become essential. You are not just "opening" your relationship; you are co-designing a new

Garden Plan, with clear boundaries, temporary rules (trellises), and sustainable agreements.

A TOUR OF OPEN RELATIONSHIP STYLES

"Open relationship" isn't a single design; it's a category containing many different approaches to tending your shared land.

- **The Annual Flower Bed (Sex-Only Openness):** This model allows for sexual experiences, but with the shared understanding that these connections are like beautiful annual flowers– planted for a season but not intended to become permanent. The No-Bullshit Reality is that you cannot legislate feelings. A smarter plan includes a pre-negotiated strategy for what to do when a temporary bloom starts to develop unexpectedly deep roots.

- **The Hidden Blight (Don't Ask, Don't Tell - DADT):** This model permits outside sexual experiences on the condition that they are never discussed. This is often born from fear–a misguided attempt to get the benefits of openness without having to face the difficult emotions it can bring up. But this practice is a hidden blight, a disease spreading unseen through the root system. It makes informed consent about sexual health impossible and poisons the soil with suspicion.

- **The Seasonal Bloom (Situational Non-Monogamy):** This model grants one-off permission for a specific event (like a festival or a work trip) or even a specific person–like a rare flower that only blooms under certain conditions. The No-Bullshit Reality is that a single encounter can have a powerful emotional echo that doesn't always feel temporary.

- **The Garden Gate Ajar (Monogamish):** This describes a fundamentally monogamous garden where the gate is left slightly ajar for small, specific, and carefully negotiated exceptions.

A CRITICAL WARNING: THE DISPOSABLE SEEDLING PROBLEM

This is a big ethical blind spot in many open relationships. The other people you connect with are whole, complex human beings, not disposable seedlings for your garden project. If your open model relies on deceiving or dehumanizing third parties, it is not ethical. Full stop.

Your ethical obligation to them includes:

- **Full Disclosure:** They have the right to know the full layout of your garden, including your relationship status and any agreements that affect them.

- **Respect for Their Humanity:** Treat them with kindness, not as a dirty secret.

- **Clean Endings:** End the connection with clarity and compassion, not by ghosting.

Case Study: The Disposable Seedling

Anna and Tom have an open relationship with a "no feelings" rule. Tom starts a casual sexual relationship with Maria. He doesn't tell her about the rule. After a few months, Maria develops feelings. Tom panics, tells Anna, and then ghosts Maria. This panic is the predictable outcome of a "no feelings" rule designed to fail. In his fear of breaking his agreement with Anna, Tom commits a profound ethical failure toward Maria.

In this scenario, Maria was treated not as a person but as a disposable seedling. An ethical approach would have required Tom to be up-front with Maria about the rule from the beginning, allowing her to consent to the terms of the garden she was entering.

NO-BULLSHIT TL;DR

- "Open relationship" is a dangerously vague label. Your job is to replace that vagueness with a specific, co-created Garden Plan (Chapter 11).

- The most common ethical failure in open relationships is treating new partners as disposable. They are whole people, not accessories to your growth.

- A "no feelings" rule is designed to fail. A "what we'll do when feelings inevitably happen" plan is a sign of wisdom and care.

- Opening a relationship is an amplifier, not a fixer. It cannot save a dying garden; it will only make the weeds grow faster.

CHAPTER 17: SOLO POLYAMORY & RELATIONSHIP ANARCHY

LOVING WITHOUT A SHARED BLUEPRINT

What if the goal of love isn't to merge two lives into one?

What if your most profound, life-sustaining connections don't fit neatly into the boxes of "partner," "lover," or "friend"? What if you want deep commitment without cohabitation, or lasting intimacy without enmeshment?

This chapter is for the fiercely independent, the philosophical radicals, and the people who have always felt that the traditional relationship escalator leads to a destination they never wanted to reach. These styles are often misunderstood, even within ENM communities, as being "less serious," "selfish," or "commitment phobic." That is bullshit. In reality, they can be some of the most intentional, self-aware, and radically honest ways to love.

THE PAIN OF THE ESCALATOR & THE FREEDOM OF THE OFF-RAMP

As we discussed in Chapter 2, the Relationship Escalator is the default script for a "successful" relationship: dating, exclusivity, moving in, merging finances, marriage. For many people, this path feels safe and desirable. But for others, it can feel like a slow-moving conveyor belt toward a life that isn't truly theirs. It can feel like a cage of "shoulds" that leaves no room for what you actually want.

Solo Polyamory and Relationship Anarchy are not just casual alternatives; they are the conscious, intentional off-ramps from that escalator. They are different paths, walked by people who have decided that their own autonomy is their true north.

SOLO POLYAMORY: THE SELF AS PRIMARY PARTNER

If couple-centric polyamory is about decentering the dyad, Solo Polyamory (SoPo) takes it a step further by re-centering the self. **Solo Polyamory** is a relationship philosophy where the individual identifies as their own primary partner.

This is a conscious choice to build a life where your own autonomy is the central foundation. A solo polyamorous person typically maintains multiple relationships, does not seek a traditional primary-style partnership that includes merging life infrastructure (like cohabitation), and prioritizes their own friendships, career, creative life, and personal space.

This is not about being single. A solo poly person can have multiple deep, committed, long-term relationships. The key distinction is the rejection of relational merging as a required goal or a measure of success.

RELATIONSHIP ANARCHY: RIPPING UP THE RULEBOOK

If solo polyamory is about getting off the escalator, Relationship Anarchy (RA) is about dynamiting the escalator factory. It's about taking the inherited rulebook of relationship categories and putting it through a shredder.

Relationship Anarchy (RA) is a radical philosophy that rejects all normative rules about how relationships "should" work. It dismantles the hierarchy between relationship types, arguing that a romantic partner is not inherently more valuable than a best friend, a creative collaborator, or a chosen family member. It advocates for building every connection from scratch based on desire, trust, and mutual consent.

In a relationship anarchist's life, the lines between "partner," "friend," and "lover" are consciously erased. Each connection is valued for what it uniquely is, not for the category it fits into.

THE NO-BULLSHIT REALITY: AUTONOMY VS. AVOIDANCE

The accusation that these philosophies are just an excuse for being "commitment-phobic" is a misunderstanding. They are a commitment to a different life structure.

However, there is a common bullshit trap to be aware of: the Autonomy Shield. Both Solo Polyamory and Relationship Anarchy can be twisted—often unconsciously—into a shield to avoid all vulnerability and accountability. This is often not a sign of malice, but a trauma response born from past relationships where enmeshment led to harm. It's an inherited script that says "closeness = suffocation."

- The "Solo Poly Avoidant" uses their identity as a reason to never be emotionally available or reliable.

- The "Anarchist Flake" uses the philosophy of "no rules" as an excuse to avoid having difficult conversations about agreements, boundaries, or the impact of their behavior on others.

The compassionate work is to differentiate between healthy autonomy and fear-based avoidance. The no-bullshit truth is that radical autonomy requires radical accountability. A healthy solo polyamorist takes full ownership of their impact; a healthy relationship anarchist is obsessed with clear, co-created consent.

THE DATING LANDSCAPE: NAVIGATING AS A SOLO PERSON

As a person practicing one of these styles, you walk into a dating world full of unexamined assumptions. You might be seen as a "threat" by insecure couples, an "easy catch" by players, or a temporary diversion by people still riding the relationship escalator.

Chapters 28 and 29 ("The Single Man" and "The Single Woman") are your essential field guides to navigating this. They will give you the tools to deal with the specific stereotypes you will face to vet partners ruthlessly for those who respect your autonomy, and to hold your boundaries with power and grace.

Table 17.1: A Comparison of Solo Polyamory and Relationship Anarchy

Feature	Solo Polyamory (SoPo)	Relationship Anarchy (RA)
Core Philosophy	I am my own primary partner.	All relationships are built from scratch with no default categories or hierarchies.
View of Hierarchy	May acknowledge some hierarchy (e.g., anchor partners) but avoids traditional primacy.	Rejects all hierarchy—romantic ≠ more valuable than platonic or chosen family.
Commitment	Committed to individuals without merging lives; values consistency and mutual respect.	Commitment is freely chosen, redefined per relationship, and not bound by cultural norms.
Common Misconception	"Afraid of commitment"	"Anti-structure, chaotic, or irresponsible"
Real Challenge	Risk of isolation; social invisibility; being misunderstood as avoidant.	Requires constant renegotiation; misunderstood by nearly all traditional frameworks.

NO-BULLSHIT TL;DR

- You can be your own primary partner. Choosing autonomy over enmeshment is a valid, powerful commitment to yourself.

- Relationship Anarchy is the practice of building every connection on its own unique terms, free from the inherited hierarchy of "partner," "friend," or "lover."

- These are not excuses to be flaky. The philosophies of autonomy can be misused to avoid accountability. Radical independence requires radical accountability.

- Not wanting to merge your life with a partner's doesn't mean you're "commitment-phobic." It means you are the conscious architect of your own life.

CHAPTER 18: PLATONIC PARTNERSHIPS

WHEN YOUR BEST FRIEND IS YOUR LIFE PARTNER

We have been sold a bill of goods.

The story goes like this: your life partner, your "One," must also be your romantic and sexual partner. Anything less—a deep bond with a best friend, a sibling, or a creative collaborator—is lovely, but it's not the main event. It's second-tier.

That is amatonormativity in action, and it is bullshit.

This chapter validates the relationships our culture devalues. It is proof that your anchor—the person you trust most in the world and want to build a life with—does not have to be your lover. Sometimes, the most profound partnership is the one that is built on a foundation of deep, unshakable platonic love.

QUEERPLATONIC PARTNERSHIPS (QPPS): A DEEPER DIVE

The term **queerplatonic partnership (QPP)** originated in communities of aromantic people (who experience little to no romantic attraction) and asexual people (who experience little to no sexual attraction). They needed a word to describe committed, emotionally intense relationships that deliberately exist outside the traditional binary of "romantic partner" or "platonic friend."

A QPP is a formal, non-romantic partnership built on a level of intimacy and commitment that our culture typically reserves for romantic couples. It often involves the tangible elements of a traditional life partnership: cohabitating, sharing finances, co-parenting, and building a shared future together.

The "queer" in queerplatonic isn't just about sexual orientation; it's about the verb: the act of "queering," which means to deliberately challenge, question, and break traditional rules. In this case, it's about breaking the rule that separates "romance" from "friendship." It's a conscious choice to take the intensity, commitment, and priority we culturally reserve for romantic partnerships and apply it to a platonic bond.

BUILDING A LIFE AROUND PLATONIC PARTNERS: THE LOGISTICS

Creating a life centered on platonic partnerships requires high intention because you are operating without a societal script.

The No-Bullshit Reality: You are not just having a deep friendship; you are consciously designing a life partnership from scratch, using the tools of intentionality and communication because the default cultural rulebook offers you nothing. This is advanced, courageous work.

- **Explicit Communication:** Because there are no default expectations, everything must be discussed. Do you want to live together? Share a bank account? What are your agreements around other partners, both romantic and platonic?

- **Legal Protections:** The legal system is designed to protect married, romantic couples. Platonic life partners must be proactive in creating their own protections through wills, healthcare proxies, and cohabitation agreements.

- **Navigating Romantic Relationships:** A common challenge is a new romantic partner feeling threatened by the intensity of the QPP. This requires radical clarity from the first date. The script is not a request but a statement of fact: "My platonic partner is my life partner. They are not a temporary roommate. Any romantic relationship I have must joyfully coexist with that fact."

- **Building Social Understanding:** You will likely need to have ongoing conversations with your wider social circle and chosen family to help them understand the seriousness of your partnership. This can mean explicitly saying, "Ben isn't just my roommate; he is my family. When you invite me to a major life event, you are inviting both of us."

Case Study: The Platonic Anchor

Amelia and Ben have been in a queerplatonic partnership for 15 years. They co-own a house and are each other's legal next-of-kin. Both date other people romantically. When Amelia starts dating a new man, she is upfront from day one: "Ben is my family. We are building a life together. A relationship with me means making space for him as a core part of my life." This clarity acts as a filter, weeding out potential partners who are unable to comprehend a life where a platonic bond holds the primary, anchor position.

Table 18.1: Commitment and Recognition Across Relationship Structures

Feature	Typical Friendship	Queerplatonic Partnership (QPP)	Romantic Partnership
Level of Commitment	Variable, often informal	High, often intended as a life partnership	High, often intended as a life partnership
Shared Infrastructure	Usually low (separate finances, homes)	Can be high (cohabitation, shared finances, co-parenting)	Often high, with the goal of merging lives and resources
Social Recognition	Low— typically seen as "just friends"	Low—often misunderstood or not taken seriously	High—legally and socially privileged and institutionally supported

NAVIGATING SOCIETAL INVISIBILITY

One of the biggest challenges of platonic-centered relationships is the constant need to explain and validate your life to a world that doesn't have a category for it. You will constantly face the assumption that your QPP is just a placeholder until you find a real (i.e., romantic) partner.

Navigating this requires a strong sense of self and a prepared "elevator pitch" for the curious but well-meaning: "We're life partners. Our connection is platonic, and it's the most important relationship in my life."

NO-BULLSHIT TL;DR

- Your most important, life-sustaining partnership does not have to be romantic or sexual.

- Queerplatonic Partnerships (QPPs) are a radical and valid challenge to the amatonormative script that prioritizes romantic love above all else.

- Building a life with a platonic partner is an act of conscious design. It requires radical honesty, proactive legal planning, and clear communication with everyone in your life.

- The person who feels like home does not have to be a romantic partner.

CHAPTER 19: ACE & ALLO IN ENM

NAVIGATING MIXED-ORIENTATION RELATIONSHIPS

In most conversations about Ethical Non-Monogamy, a central assumption hums quietly in the background: that everyone involved is seeking sexual connection.

But what happens when, for one or more people in the relationship network, sex isn't the primary driver? What if it's not a driver at all?

Welcome to the world of mixed-orientation relationships, specifically those between **asexual** (or "ace") individuals, who experience little to no intrinsic sexual attraction, and **allosexual** ("allo") individuals, who do. Navigating this dynamic within ENM requires a level of creativity, compassion, and communication that can be challenging but also profoundly rewarding. It forces us to deconstruct our assumptions about what intimacy truly is. This chapter is not just for people in ace/allo relationships; it is for anyone who wants to master the art of building intimacy in all its forms. It is a deep dive into one of the most radical and freeing ideas in all of ENM: that sex and intimacy are not the same thing.

BEYOND THE DEFINITION: ASEXUALITY IN PRACTICE

Asexuality is an orientation, not a choice or a medical problem. It exists on a broad spectrum, which includes identities like **demisexual** (experiencing sexual attraction only after a strong emotional bond has formed). Some ace people are sex-repulsed, some are sex-indifferent, and some are sex-favorable, meaning they may enjoy the act of sex for reasons other than personal sexual desire (like for a partner's pleasure).

When an ace person and an allo person are in a relationship, the core challenge is not a lack of love, but a potential mismatch in their needs for sexual expression. In a monogamous context, this often leads to a painful dynamic: the allo partner feels rejected, and the ace partner feels broken or pressured. In theory, ethical non-monogamy can offer a beautiful solution.

Ethical non-monogamy can, in theory, offer a beautiful solution. It creates the possibility for the allosexual partner to have their sexual needs met with other partners, while freeing the ace partner from the pressure of being the sole source of that intimacy. This preserves the deep, loving bond they do share, but it requires dismantling one of the core assumptions of the Monogamy Mindset: that a relationship without sex is somehow less valid or "real."

DESIRE VS. INTIMACY: DECOUPLING SEX FROM VALUE

The central task for an ace/allo ENM partnership is to consciously decouple sex from value. This means intentionally separating the concepts of sex, desire, and intimacy, and refusing to rank them in a hierarchy of importance.

Table 19.1: Decoupling Sex, Desire, and Intimacy

Concept	What It IS (Definition)	What It IS NOT (Common Misconception)
Sex	A specific physical act that can be shared for pleasure, play, or connection	A mandatory part of a loving relationship or the ultimate proof of intimacy
Desire	The internal experience of wanting someone sexually or romantically	A reflection of how much someone loves or is committed to their primary partner
Intimacy	The experience of deep connection, emotional vulnerability, and mutual closeness	Something that only exists or matters when it's tied to sexual activity

An ace/allo ENM partnership must tear this bundle apart. It must build a foundation on the understanding that an allo partner's desire for sex with another person is not a reflection on the value of their relationship with their ace partner. An ace partner's lack of sexual desire does not mean a lack of love.

Case Study: Building a Balanced Agreement

Consider Leo (allo) and Maya (ace). They have a deep, loving partnership, but they open their relationship to allow Leo to explore sexual connections. Their agreement is built on two pillars:

- **Prioritizing Leo and Maya's Intimacy:** They schedule dedicated, non-sexual date nights focused on emotional and sensual connection. They explicitly talk about what makes each of them feel loved and desired outside of a sexual context.

- **Radical Honesty about Leo's Other Connections:** Leo is open with his other partners about his relationship structure, making it clear that Maya is his nesting and romantic partner. He practices safer sex and communicates openly.

This works because they have successfully separated sex from the hierarchy of importance. Leo's sexual relationships are a valid part of his life, but they do not devalue the deep, non-sexual intimacy he shares with Maya.

NAVIGATING THE "ROADBLOCK" DYNAMIC: COMMON PITFALLS

For the allosexual partner: You may feel guilty for "needing" sex outside your relationship or feel like your desires are a burden on your ace partner.

For the asexual partner: You may internalize the societal message that you are "broken" or a "roadblock" to your partner's happiness. This is especially challenging when your partner is experiencing a form of intimacy with someone else that you cannot or do not want to provide.

These painful internal monologues are rarely our own original thoughts. They are the echoes of the inherited scripts we've been taught our whole lives—the ones that tell the allo partner their needs are a burden, and the ace partner that they are "broken."

> *An allo partner's internal monologue: I feel like such an asshole. I love Maya more than anything, but after my date with Kim, my body just feels… alive. And then I come home, and the guilt hits me like a truck. Am I a monster for needing this?*

> *An ace partner's internal monologue: Leo says he had a great time, and I'm happy for him. I really am. But there's this ugly voice in my head that whispers, 'She gives him something you can't. You're broken. He's going to realize he's happier with her.'*

The solution to these challenges is the hard, worthwhile work of writing a new script together—one built on relentless, compassionate communication and a shared commitment to honoring each other's realities without judgment.

NO-BULLSHIT TL;DR

- Ace/allo relationships are a valid and powerful part of the ENM landscape. A mismatch in sexual desire is not a mismatch in love.

- Decouple sex from value. This is the core skill. Intimacy is the goal, and it comes in many forms. A partner's desire for sex with others is not a judgment on you.

- ENM can provide a beautiful framework where everyone's needs are met, but it requires radical honesty, deep trust, and relentless compassion.

- Consciously design agreements that honor all forms of intimacy—sensual, emotional, intellectual—to create a structure that is nourishing for everyone.

CHAPTER 20: KINK & POWER DYNAMICS

WHEN CONSENT GETS COMPLEX

Not all ENM is kinky. Not all kinksters are non-monogamous. But let's be real: the Venn diagram of these two communities has a massive, pulsating overlap. Both are worlds for people who have decided the default scripts are not for them. If ENM is about redesigning the blueprint of your relational landscape, kink is about exploring its most profound and intense psychological terrain.

This chapter is your foundational guide to that intersection. Before we dive in, let's get our vocabulary straight, because clear language is the bedrock of consent.

- **Kink**: A broad umbrella term for non-conventional sexualities, desires, and practices. If it's not the standard script of what our culture calls vanilla sex (think missionary position, maybe some light oral sex before the main event), it probably falls under the kink umbrella. This can be anything from a partner whispering dirty talk in your ear to elaborate role-playing fantasies.

- **BDSM:** A major subset of kink. The acronym stands for three distinct but often overlapping categories of play. This isn't just about black leather and dungeons; it's a huge spectrum of human expression. Let's break down what these actually look like in practice:

- **Bondage & Discipline (B&D):** This is about the consensual use of physical restraint and the negotiation of rules.

- **Bondage** can be as gentle as holding someone's wrists down during sex or using silk scarves to tie them to a headboard. It can also be as intense as a full-body suspension with intricate rope art.

- *Discipline* is about creating a structure of rules for a scene. A pre-negotiated consequence for breaking a rule might be getting spanked, writing lines ("I will be a good girl/boy/pet"), or being made to kneel in a corner. These consequences are part of the play itself.

- **Dominance & Submission (D/s):** This is about the consensual exchange of power and authority, which is often more psychological than physical.

    o **Dominance** is the act of taking on the power role, guiding the scene, and taking responsibility for a partner's well-being.

    o **Submission** is the act of consensually and temporarily surrendering control to a trusted partner. This can be as simple as a partner saying, "For the next hour, you're in charge, tell me what to do," or as profound as a 24/7 power-exchange dynamic.

- **Sadism & Masochism (S&M):** This is about the consensual exchange of sensation—often pain that is experienced as pleasure.

  o **Sadism** is deriving pleasure from giving consensual sensation.

  o **Masochism** is deriving pleasure from receiving it. This is a massive spectrum. It can be the sharp sting of a hand on a butt, the rhythmic thud of a flogger across the back, the bite of a whip on the thigh, the pinch of a clothespin on a nipple, or the intensity of hot wax play.

- **Kink-shaming:** The act of judging, mocking, or pathologizing someone for their kinky desires. It is a form of bullying, and it has no place in an ethical community. This book operates from a place of kink-positivity.

This chapter is not a how-to manual for specific acts. It is a no-bullshit guide to the ethics and mindset required to engage with kink safely. Kink is not about the whip; it's about the incredible trust that allows the whip to be held.

A CRITICAL WARNING: THIS IS NOT A THING YOU WING

Before we go any further: Ethical kink is not something you improvise. Unlike vanilla sex, where culture gives us flawed (but existing) scripts, ethical kink has no default setting. Every single interaction must be built from scratch with education, caution, and meticulous communication. Ignorance is not an excuse; it's a liability that can cause real, lasting harm.

THE NO-BULLSHIT TRUTH ABOUT POWER

To an outsider, kink—especially BDSM—can look like a simulation of abuse. This is the most profound misunderstanding of all. In fact, ethical kink is the exact opposite of abuse.

Abuse is the act of taking power that isn't yours. Ethical power exchange is the act of consensually, and temporarily, gifting a power you absolutely possess.

It is a conscious exploration of power dynamics, allowing people to reclaim their agency, explore their desires, and experience a level of intimacy that vanilla interactions rarely touch.

THE SACRED TOOLKIT: KINK'S MASTERCLASS IN CONSENT

To navigate this intense psychological landscape, the kink community has developed a sophisticated ethical framework that is a masterclass in consent. These are the sacred, non-negotiable practices that create the container for safe, transformative exploration.

The Scene: The Power of the Container

At the heart of ethical kink is the concept of a scene: a pre-negotiated, time-bound container for kink activities. It has a clear beginning, a middle, and an end. This reframes consent not as a blanket state, but as something granted for a specific activity, for a specific duration. The consent you give to be spanked during a thirty-minute scene on a Saturday night does not roll over. Consent is not a subscription service; it expires.

Negotiation: The Architecture of Trust

In ethical kink, you do not "wing it." You negotiate. This is the conversation where partners discuss desires, limits, and safewords before play begins. A good negotiation is meticulously detailed, covering everything from physical acts to emotional needs and safety protocols.

The result of this negotiation is often called a **protocol**. This is the collection of pre-agreed rules, rituals, and behaviors that structure the dynamic for the scene. For example, a protocol might state that a submissive must kneel when their Dominant enters the room, or that they will only speak when spoken to during the scene. It is the mutually-designed script that allows both partners to feel safe enough to play.

CONSENT DURING PLAY: THE ART OF ESCALATION & SAFEWORDS

Kink at its best understands that consent is an ongoing process.

- **Checking In:** An ethical Dominant is constantly attuned to their submissive's state, checking in verbally ("How are you feeling?") and non-verbally.

- **Safewords:** This is the sacred brake pedal. The most common tool is the traffic light system:

- **"Green light"** is a verbal check-in response meaning, "I'm good, everything feels great, continue or even escalate."

- **"Yellow light"** is a safeword meaning, "Slow down, check in, something is becoming too intense or needs adjustment." It's a call for caution.

- **"Red light"** is a safeword meaning, "Stop immediately, end the scene now, no questions asked." This is a hard, non-negotiable stop.

While this is the most common system, you'll encounter variations. The specific tool doesn't matter; what matters is that it is pre-negotiated and instantly respected. Ignoring a safeword is not part of the scene; it is assault.

Aftercare: The Practice of Gentle Re-entry

This is perhaps the most profound practice the kink world has to offer. Aftercare is the *mandatory* process of emotional and physical support that follows a scene. After an intense experience, you don't just get up and leave. You tend to each other. This can look like cuddling, getting a glass of water, or simply being quietly present together. It is the practice of gently guiding each other back from that intense landscape and reaffirming the care and trust that made the journey possible.

WEAVING KINK INTO MULTIPLE RELATIONSHIPS

Combining these dynamics with ENM requires extraordinarily high levels of communication and compartmentalization. Common tension points include:

- **Protocol Bleed**: When the rules or dynamics of a kink relationship seep into a vanilla relationship without consent.

- **Aftercare Black Holes:** When a partner outsources the essential labor of aftercare to an uninvolved partner, burdening them with the emotional fallout of a scene they didn't participate in.

- **Hierarchical Jealousy:** When a vanilla partner feels threatened by the unique and profound intimacy of their partner's D/s dynamic.

- **Consent Confusion:** The dangerous trap where a Dominant mistakenly believes their authority extends to their submissive's other partners.

Case Study in Complex Dynamics: Ethical Cuckolding

The term "cuckold" is often used as a playground insult, but within the world of ethical kink, it describes a complex and intense dynamic. In its modern, consensual form, a **cuckold** (male) or **cuckquean** (female) is a person who derives pleasure—often intensely erotic—from their partner having sexual encounters with others.

The No-Bullshit Reality: This is not simply a partner who is "okay" with non-monogamy. It is an advanced kink dynamic that intentionally plays with intense psychological elements. It requires the absolute highest levels of trust and security in the primary relationship, and often involves a unique form of consensual power exchange. The dynamic can be a profound exploration of compersion, envy, and sometimes, consensual humiliation, where the partner's "cuckolding" is a central part of the shared erotic story. Because of its potential for emotional harm if done poorly, it requires the meticulous negotiation, consent, and aftercare central to all ethical kink.

A FINAL WARNING: WHEN KINK BECOMES A MASK FOR ABUSE

Just as the term "poly" can be used to excuse bad behavior, the language and aesthetics of kink can be the perfect shield for an abuser. Each of these red flags represents a corruption of one of kink's core ethical principles.

Watch out for these massive red flags:

- The Unaccountable Dom: A person who claims the title but refuses responsibility for the well-being of their submissive(s). They see submission as a right, not a gift.

- Using a Dynamic to Isolate: A partner insists that because of your D/s protocol, you cannot see friends or other partners who "don't understand your dynamic." This is a classic isolation tactic.

- "It's Part of the Scene": A classic abuser's excuse, used to justify behavior that is genuinely harmful, non-consensual, or outside the bounds of the initial negotiation.

- Punishing "Out-of-Role" Dissent: You always have the right to pause the dynamic and speak as an equal partner. If doing so is met with punishment, that is not D/s; it is abuse.

If it feels like control, if you feel afraid, and if you don't feel safe to say no, it's not a healthy power exchange. It's a trap.

Table 20.1: Ethical Kink vs. Abusive Behavior

Element	Ethical Kink	Abusive Behavior
Power	A consensual gift, explicitly negotiated and clearly limited	Unchecked control, framed as a right or entitlement
Consent	Enthusiastic, informed, and ongoing; can be revoked at any time with a safeword	Coerced or manipulated; safewords are ignored or dissent is punished
Rules/ Protocol	A mutually designed framework to enhance play and connection	A mechanism for control, used to isolate or dominate outside of negotiated scenes
Pain	A negotiated sensation given or received for shared pleasure and trust	Harm inflicted without consent or used as retribution or control

NO-BULLSHIT TL;DR

- Ethical kink is not about the act itself; it is a practice of radical trust, conscious vulnerability, and meticulous communication.

- The core of ethical power exchange is that power is a temporary, consensual gift, not a right.

- The "Holy Trinity" of Negotiation, Safewords, and Aftercare are the sacred, non-negotiable tools that make safe exploration possible.

- Kink is never an excuse for abuse. Any dynamic that erodes your autonomy or isolates you from your support system is not kink; it's control.

PART 4: LIFE IN PRACTICE

CHAPTER 21: THE DIGITAL WORLD

SWIPING, VETTING, & SURVIVING WITH INTEGRITY

So, you've done the internal work, talked with your partners, and designed your approach. Now comes the first test. This is where your ethics meet the algorithm. For most, the journey into ENM begins in the digital world: a landscape of dating apps, social media groups, and online forums. This world offers incredible opportunities for connection. It is also a minefield of timewasters, ethical pitfalls, and people who use "ENM" as a synonym for "I don't want to be accountable."

This is your guide to navigating the digital territory without losing your values, your boundaries, or your goddamn mind.

YOUR PROFILE: THE FIRST ACT OF INTEGRITY

Your profile isn't just an advertisement; it's your primary filtering tool. A lazy profile attracts lazy people. A thoughtful profile attracts thoughtful people. Above all, it must be honest.

- **Your Relationship Structure:** Be explicit. "Married and opening up" is a start, but "Hierarchically partnered, we date separately" is better. "Solo polyamorous" tells people you are your own primary.

- **What You Are Seeking:** "Fun" is not enough. Are you seeking casual play partners, a committed secondary relationship, a queerplatonic partner, a regular BDSM dynamic?

- **Key Boundaries and Logistics:** This is non-negotiable. State your capacity upfront. "I can date one evening a week," or "I am a parent, so my schedule is limited." This manages expectations from the very first click.

Case Study: Vague vs. No-Bullshit Profiles

There isn't one "right" way to write a profile, but there is a wrong way. The wrong way is vague and self-centered. A good profile, regardless of its style, is clear, honest, and respectful of the reader's time.

- **The Vague Profile (Avoid This):** "Married and new to this. Looking for a fun, drama-free girl to join us for adventures. See where things go!"

  Analysis: *This is a classic unicorn-hunting profile. "Drama-free" is a red flag that often means "have no needs that inconvenience us." "See where things go" is ambiguous and signals a lack of clear intention.*

- **No-Bullshit Profile: The Direct & Serious:** "Ethically non-monogamous. I'm married with a wonderful nesting partner (we date separately) and am seeking a committed secondary partner for regular dates and deep connection. Due to family commitments, I can typically offer one evening a week. My integrity, communication, and your safety are my top priorities."

> **Analysis:** *This profile is direct, clear, and uses the community's language. It's perfect for someone who wants to attract experienced ENM practitioners looking for a serious connection.*

- **No-Bullshit Profile: The Warm & Playful:** "Happily partnered, exploring solo connections. I'm a big fan of board games, long hikes, and dive bar trivia nights. Looking for a fun, kinky, and kind person for regular dates and shenanigans. Life is busy, so scheduling in advance is my love language. If you're a good communicator who doesn't take themselves too seriously, let's talk!"

> **Analysis:** *This profile is equally effective. It communicates the same core information (partnered, dating solo, limited time) but does so with a more playful, personality-driven voice. It will attract people who are drawn to that specific energy.*

A FIELD GUIDE TO ENM CONNECTION PLATFORMS

Each platform has its own culture and risks.

- **Feeld:** The current front-runner for the ENM, queer, and kink-curious. Its design encourages upfront expression of desires. The transparency is a major plus, but its reputation also attracts "poly-curious" individuals who are enthusiastic but may not have done the work.

- **OkCupid:** A personality-focused platform with a questionnaire that can find matches based on deeper compatibility. The trade-off is its mainstream user base; you'll spend more time filtering out people seeking monogamy.

- **#Open:** Built for the ENM community, its features and hashtag system (#RelationshipAnarchy, #KitchenTablePoly) are designed for those who already speak the language. Its main challenge is often a smaller user base.

- **Bumble and Tinder:** The mainstream giants. Finding ENM connections here requires a different strategy. Be ruthlessly efficient: state "Ethically Non-Monogamous" in the first line of your profile as a filter.

- **Reddit:** This is not a dating app; it is a collection of anonymous forums, and it can be highly dangerous. Anonymous forums are not communities; they are crowds. Reddit is built on total anonymity with throwaway accounts, making it a breeding ground for scammers and predators. Use it for information, but be extremely cautious when moving from public forums to private messages.

DIGITAL LIFE: ETHICS, SAFETY, & ETIQUETTE

How you handle privacy, trust, and safety online is a direct reflection of your character.

The High-Stakes Art of Exchanging Nudes

- **Never Demand, Only Invite.** A respectful invitation makes "no" a safe answer.

- **You Owe No One a Photo.** Do not feel pressured to send a nude just because you received one. This is a common tactic used by scammers.

- **Treat Received Nudes Like a Sacred Trust.** If someone sends you an explicit photo, you have been handed their vulnerability. It is not yours to share.

- **Honor the Deletion Request.** If someone asks you to delete a nude of them, the only ethical response is "yes," immediately and without argument. Their right to control their intimate image and feel safe supersedes your right to keep a copy.

- **Send Smart.** Remember that once a photo is sent, you lose control of it forever. Consider cropping your face or identifying features.

Community Conduct: Privacy, Consent, and Discretion

- **Do Not DM Without an Invitation.** Just because you are in a group together does not mean you have consent to slide into someone's private messages. Engage with them publicly in the group first. If they seem receptive, you can ask publicly or in a comment, "Would it be okay if I sent you a DM?" An unsolicited DM is almost always an unwelcome intrusion.

- **No Recording Without Explicit Consent.** You do not take a picture or record a video of anyone without their clear permission.

- **Consent to Record is NOT Consent to Share.** Someone's excitement to make a private video with you is not permission for you to share it with anyone else.

- **Treat Event Chats as Public Spaces.** Assume any pre-party group chat could be screenshotted and leaked.

- **Respect Group Boundaries.** Do not cross-post events from other groups without permission from the admins.

- **Outing is a Betrayal.** What you see on the apps, stays on the apps. Outing someone can cost them their job, housing, and family. Your silence is their safety.

- **Elevate the Conversation.** Do not fill community spaces with low-effort "thirst posts" or tacky memes, there are groups for that.

The Fantasy vs. Reality Trap: Navigating Online Chemistry

- **Flirting is Not Consent.** Just because someone is engaging in hot chat does not mean they have consented to meet you.

- **Fantasy is Not a Proposition.** Sharing a fantasy with you is not the same as inviting you to fulfill it. If you are unsure, clarify with respect: "This is a lot of fun. Just so I'm clear, are we just having a good time talking, or are you hoping to explore this in person?"

- **Beware the Fantasy Bond.** It is easy to build an intense connection with an idealized version of a person online. We've been trained by a thousand romantic comedies to fall for a curated highlight reel. This "fantasy bond" is a powerful illusion that often shatters upon contact with their real, flawed, human self.

The goal of early online chatting is not to build a fantasy; it's to gather enough data to see if a real-world meeting is worth the time.

Vetting Your Digital Environment

- **Vet Your Groups.** Do not join communities that do not vet their members. A good admin team will have a screening process.

- **Vet Your Friend Requests.** Be deeply skeptical of unsolicited requests, even from profiles with mutual friends who may have been duped.

NO-BULLSHIT TL;DR

- Your profile is your first act of integrity. Be ruthlessly honest about who you are, what you're seeking, and your real-world capacity.

- Practice impeccable digital ethics. Protect people's privacy, honor their boundaries, and never assume consent.

- Ground online chemistry in real life. The goal of texting is to schedule a vetting date, not to build a fantasy bond with a stranger.

- Your digital conduct is your character in public. Be a person of integrity, even when you think no one is watching.

CHAPTER 22: THE FIRST STEPS

FROM THE SCREEN TO THE SCENE

You've done it. You've navigated the digital world, crafted a profile, survived the DMs, and now it's time for the most important and often most nerve-wracking step: meeting in person. The transition from online chemistry to real-world interaction is where theory becomes practice. It's where you discover if the person who was witty and charming in text is someone you actually enjoy sharing oxygen with.

This chapter is your guide to the first, crucial steps into the physical world. It's about mastering the art of the low-stakes first meeting—the vetting date and the community munch. Get this part right, and you set yourself up for success. Rush it, and you're setting yourself up for a world of preventable heartache.

THE VETTING DATE: YOUR MOST IMPORTANT FIRST MEETING

Let's be clear: the first in-person meeting is not a "first date." It is a **vetting meeting**. Its purpose is not romance or seduction, but data collection, risk assessment, and an act of profound self-care. You are investing a small amount of time and energy to protect yourself from a world of preventable heartache.

You are there to answer one fundamental question: Is this person who they presented themselves to be, and do I feel safe and respected in their presence?

The Logistics of a Safe Vetting Date

- **Public and Neutral:** Meet in a public place where you can easily leave. A coffee shop is ideal. Do not agree to meet at their home or have them pick you up. Maintain control of your own transportation and your own exit.

- **Time-Bound:** Keep it short. An hour is plenty of time. Having another appointment to get to (even a fictional one) can be a useful tool for ensuring a clean exit.

- **Sober (or Close to It):** You need your wits about you to accurately assess the other person, your environment, and your own feelings.

- **No play on the first meet.** This is a non-negotiable community safety standard. The vetting meeting is for conversation only. Anyone who pressures you for a physical hookup is showing you a massive red flag.

The Art of Vetting: What to Look For

Your vetting date is about collecting data. You're not just looking for red flags; you're looking for alignment and a sense of safety. Pay attention to:

- **The Vibe Check:** Your nervous system has been learning to detect bullshit for your entire life; it is often smarter than your conscious mind, which can be easily fooled by a charming smile or the script you want to believe. Trust your gut. If something feels off, it is. "The vibe was off" is a complete and valid reason to decline a second date.

- **A Warning for the "Out of Practice" Dater:** If you are coming out of a long-term monogamous relationship, this may be your first "first date" in twenty years. Be aware of this. You are used to seeing your partner at their messiest and most authentic. A new person is putting on a performance. They are showing you their highlight reel. The "but they seemed so nice" trap is easy to fall into when you've forgotten how charming a curated first impression can be. Your job is to remember that you do not know this person. This is also why a "vouch" from a trusted friend is so valuable—it provides data beyond the performance. Just make sure the friend who is vouching for them really knows them, beyond just seeing them at parties. Be curious, be open, but be skeptical.

- **Listen to How They Talk About Others.** The way a person speaks about people who are not in the room is the best preview you will ever get of how they will one day speak about you.

- **The "Mentor" Couple (A Major Yellow Flag):** Be wary of established couples who primarily date "newbies," framing it as a generous offer to "show you the ropes." This is a **yellow flag**. It could be genuine, but it could also be a predatory search for a blank slate they can mold to their rules. The core question you must investigate is: **Are they looking for an equal partner, or a compliant student?**

- **Ask Good Questions (Like a Human).** This isn't an interrogation. Weave your questions into the flow of conversation.

- To understand their capacity: "So, what does your ideal week look like when it comes to balancing time with your different partners and your own life?"

- To open the safer sex talk: "Since we're both meeting new people, I like to be up-front about sexual health. For me, that means [your practice here]. What does that look like for you?"

- To clarify definitions: "I saw on your profile you're looking for something casual. I'm curious, what does 'casual' actually look and feel like for you?"

THE MUNCH: THE COMMUNITY'S LIVING ROOM

After a few vetting meetings, you might be ready to find your people. A **munch** is a low-key, non-sexual social gathering, usually held in a public place. It is the safest and most common entry point into a local ENM community.

How to Find a Munch

- **FetLife (The Essential, Unvetted Hub):** For better or for worse, the primary hub for finding local munches and kink events is FetLife. Think of it as a specialized social media platform for the kink and ENM communities. You will need to create a profile to access its groups and event listings.

- **A No-Bullshit Warning:** You must understand that FetLife is **not a dating site, and it is not a vetted space.** There is no real verification process. A person with a decade-old profile covered in glowing "recommendations" from friends could still be a known predator in their local scene. Do not mistake online popularity for trustworthiness.

- Treat every interaction on FetLife with the same caution you would on any other public social media site. Use it as a tool to *find* public, low-stakes events like munches. Do not use it to find private play partners until you are deeply integrated into a local, trusted community. A profile on FetLife is not a background check; it is just a profile. Your real-world vetting is what will keep you safe.

- **Meetup.com & Facebook Groups:** In some cities, you can find public ENM social groups on more mainstream platforms. Search for "polyamory," "ethical non-monogamy," or "ENM" in your city.

- **Vet the Munch Itself:** Before you go, look at the event description. A well-run munch will have a clear set of rules about behavior, privacy, and consent. It will have an active and communicative host. An event with a vague description or an unresponsive host is a yellow flag.

What to Expect When You Walk In (The Vibe)

Your first munch can be terrifying. You're walking into a room of strangers to talk about your non-traditional love life. Here's the reality: it will not look like a secret society or a decadent Roman orgy. It will look like a group of people at a coffee shop or a casual restaurant. You'll likely see a mix of ages, professions, and styles—people who could just as easily be at a book club or a board game meetup.

The conversation will ebb and flow. For ten minutes, everyone might be deep in a conversation about managing jealousy. The next ten minutes, they might be arguing about the latest season of a popular TV show. It's okay if you don't have anything to add to the ENM-specific talk. Just be a friendly, engaged person.

Etiquette for Your First Munch

- **Find the Host:** When you arrive, find the event organizer. Introduce yourself, mention that it's your first time, and thank them for hosting. They can often help break the ice and introduce you to a few friendly regulars.

- **Listen More Than You Speak:** In your first few munches, your primary job is to be a good guest and a quiet observer. Get a feel for the group's culture, inside jokes, and dynamics.

- **Ask Questions:** People are generally happy to share their experiences. Good opening lines are simple: "So, how did you get into ENM?" or "What's been your biggest challenge or your biggest joy with this so far?"

- **Respect Privacy:** While munches are a place to talk about ENM, don't press people for the intimate details of their sex lives. And remember the sacred rule of discretion: what you hear at the munch, and who you see at the munch, stays at the munch.

THE NEWCOMER'S DILEMMA: NAVIGATING SOCIAL PRESSURE & SELF-DISCLOSURE

When you are new, lonely, and longing to find your people, you are uniquely vulnerable. This is not a weakness; it is a sign of your beautiful, human need for belonging. But that very need can be a powerful force that leads you to override your own better judgment.

The Pressure to Say "Yes"

You're at your first munch, and one of the established community "elders" starts hitting on you. You're not really feeling it, but a voice in your head says, "If I turn them down, will I be seen as a prude? Will I be ostracized before I even get in? Maybe I should just say yes to show I'm cool."

This is a trap. It is baited with your own need for belonging. A healthy community will respect your "no." A community that penalizes you for having boundaries is not a community; it's a clique with an entry fee, and that fee is your autonomy. Your right to say "no" is not something you earn by being popular. It is your inherent right.

The Perils of Oversharing

On the flip side, in your excitement to finally be in a place where you can talk openly, it can be tempting to share everything—the details of your messy divorce, your specific kink interests, your full relationship history—with the first friendly person you meet.

Pace your self-disclosure. You are still talking to a stranger. Your personal story is valuable. Don't give it away for free. Share enough to connect, but hold back the deeper, more vulnerable parts until you have a better sense of who you are talking to. This isn't about being dishonest; it's about being safe.

NO-BULLSHIT TL;DR

- The first meeting is a vetting meeting, not a first date. Your only goals are data collection and risk assessment. Keep it short, public, sober, and with no expectation of play.

- A munch is the community's living room, not its bedroom. It's a platonic space for making friends and finding community.

- A healthy community respects your "no." A group that pressures you to say "yes" to fit in is not a community; it's a clique, and the price of admission is your autonomy.

- Pace your self-disclosure. Your personal story is valuable. Don't give it away for free until trust has been earned.

CHAPTER 23: THE SOCIAL SCENE

NAVIGATING IN-PERSON SPACES WITH INTEGRITY

So, maybe you've had a few vetting dates—some good, some awkward. Maybe you've found your footing at a local munch, or maybe you've decided it's not for you. Whatever your path has been so far, you might now be looking at the next layer of the social world: the parties, clubs, and community events. This is a different landscape. It's where the energy gets higher, the social dynamics get more complex, and the stakes for your safety and reputation get bigger.

These spaces, from intimate house parties to professional dungeons, all run on a shared foundation of consent and respect. However, each has its own unique culture, risks, and etiquette. This is your comprehensive guide to navigating the entire social scene with safety, confidence, and integrity.

THE UNIVERSAL RULES OF PLAY SPACES

Whether you are in a private home or a commercial club, a safe space is not an accident; It is co-created by everyone in it. These are not just rules from a rulebook; they are the living, breathing agreements that form the foundation of a culture of consent and trust. This is how we agree to keep each other safe.

- **Consent is Everything.** This is the prime directive. Never assume. Always ask.

- **Handle Rejection with Grace.** "No, thank you" is a complete sentence.

- **Your Body is Not the Price of Admission.** You do not owe anyone—other guests or the host—sex to justify being there. An invitation is an act of hospitality, not a transaction where you pay with sexual access.

- **A Host Who Breaks Their Own Rules is Not Safe.** The rules of the space apply to the host most of all. A host who preaches consent but gets pushy, or who violates their own stated rules on substances, is a danger. Your safest move is not to confront them directly, but to quietly leave and warn the community afterward.

- **Be a Good Bystander.** If you see something that looks off, check in with the person or alert the host. A safe community is everyone's responsibility.

- **This is a Party, Not Your Personal Dating Pool.** Be a good social mixer. Don't monopolize one person for the entire night. If you feel a strong connection, get their number for a proper date.

Common Desires and Roles: Voyeurs & Exhibitionists

As you navigate play spaces, you'll notice that not everyone is actively participating in the same way. Two of the most common and valid roles you'll encounter are voyeurism and exhibitionism.

- A **Voyeur** is someone who derives pleasure from watching others engage in sexual activity.

- An **Exhibitionist** is someone who derives pleasure from being watched.

The No-Bullshit Reality: These are not passive roles; they are active forms of participation that are still governed by consent. Ethical voyeurism means respecting the privacy of a scene and never assuming you have permission to watch; look for cues that spectators are welcome or ask from a respectful distance. Ethical exhibitionism means being aware of your surroundings and not forcing your activities on those who do not wish to be an audience.

A TOUR OF VENUES: FROM PRIVATE HOMES TO PUBLIC SPACES

The House Party Scene

The house party is the backbone of the ENM social world. It's a high-trust environment that runs on the integrity of its host and guests. Being a good guest is about more than just showing up. It's about being a responsible, respectful, and additive member of a temporary community. **It's how you get invited back.**

- **Contribute to the Cause.** Hosting is a significant act of labor and expense. If the host asks guests to chip in via Venmo or to bring a dish or a bottle to share, do it. Don't show up empty-handed. Contributing is a basic sign of respect for the host's work and generosity.

- **Respect the Host's Space and Rules.** Their house, their rules. This is the absolute law. It means you don't wander into a bedroom with a closed door. You clean up your own cups. You adhere to their stated policies on phones and substances. A host has opened their sanctuary to you; treat it with care.

- **Your Plus-One is Your Responsibility.** You do not bring a guest to a private party without the host's explicit, enthusiastic, pre-approved permission. Full stop. Never show up with an unannounced guest. A good host has carefully curated their guest list for the safety of everyone in their home.

When you ask to bring someone, you are personally **vouching** for them. You are putting your own reputation on the line and guaranteeing that this person understands the ethical framework of this world—not the inherited scripts of the vanilla dating scene. Be incredibly careful about bringing "tourists" (curious but uneducated people) into these vulnerable spaces. Their ignorance about consent culture, even if not malicious, can cause real harm. If your guest behaves badly, you have endangered the space, and it is your reputation that is on the line.

For Hosts: The Sacred Responsibility of Creating Safe Space

Opening your home to the community is an incredible act of generosity. It also comes with a profound ethical responsibility. A good party isn't about the snacks or the playlist; it's about creating a container where every guest feels safe enough to be vulnerable, connect, and play. Your home, for one night, becomes a sanctuary.

The Host's Checklist: Before the First Guest Arrives

1. **Be Explicit in Your Invitation.** This is the number one rule of ethical hosting. Do not be vague or "coy" about the nature of your event. Your invitation is an act of consent, and your guests deserve to be fully informed.

- **Bad:** "Come over for a fun get-together with like-minded people!" (This is a recipe for the "Bait-and-Switch" disaster).

- **Good:** Clearly state the nature and expectations of the event. Is it a "potluck and board games social"? A "sexy cocktail party with a clothes-off optional playroom"? Or a "hardcore, kinky play party"? Being explicit prevents misunderstandings and ensures that everyone who shows up has enthusiastically consented to the environment.

2. **Vet Your Guest List.** You are the gatekeeper to the sanctuary. Your first responsibility is to the safety of the people who have already put their trust in you. This means you do not run a public, "open-door" event.

- Only invite people you know and trust.

- For people you don't know personally, require a "vouch" from a trusted member of the community. A vouch is not just, "Oh, they're cool." It is a friend putting their own social reputation on the line and confirming that the new person is safe, understands consent, and is not a known problem in the community.

  3. **Set and Announce the Rules.** Don't make people guess the rules of your space. A good host is a clear leader. Include a concise list of your house rules in the invitation and consider posting them in a visible area of your home. This should cover:

- **Consent:** "Enthusiastic consent is required for everything. 'No' is a complete answer. 'Maybe' is a 'no'. If you are unsure, ask."

- **Play Spaces:** "Play is welcome in the downstairs playroom and the blue bedroom. The rest of the house, including the kitchen, is for social, clothed conversation."

- **Phones/Photos:** "For everyone's privacy, there is a strict no-photo/no-phone policy in play spaces."

- **Substances:** "We will have wine and beer. Please consume responsibly. No hard drugs."

  4. **Designate a Sober Point of Contact.** As the host, you may want to drink and socialize. It is a best practice to designate at least one person—you or a trusted friend—to remain sober or mostly sober for the entire event. This person should be announced or

easily identifiable. They are the designated, clear-headed go-to for any issues, from a consent violation to someone simply feeling overwhelmed and needing a quiet space or help getting a ride home. This is a profound act of community care.

Common Issue: The "Bait-and-Switch" Party

You are invited to a game night and walk into an orgy. **You are in complete control.** It is always okay to just watch (with permission), and it is always okay to leave.

Commercial Venues: Clubs and Dungeons

These are spaces where you pay an entry fee to play in a professionally managed environment. For many, the clear rules and presence of staff make this a safer and less intimidating way to explore than a private house party.

- **How to Find and Vet Them:** The safest way is through word-of-mouth at your local munch. The regulars will know the reputation of every club in your area. Before you go, scrutinize their website. A good club is proud of its safety rules and will feature its Code of Conduct prominently. A venue that hides its rules or has a vague policy on consent is a massive red flag.

- **The Vetting Process:** A good club will not just let anyone walk in off the street. Expect a vetting process, and embrace it—it's what keeps the community safe. This may involve a detailed membership application, a requirement to be sponsored by a current member, or a mandatory "first-timers" tour before the main party begins. Always take the tour. It's your best opportunity to see the space, learn the rules, and meet the staff in a low-pressure environment.

- **Club Vibe vs. Dungeon Vibe:** While both are commercial play spaces, they often have very different cultures. Lifestyle/Swingers Clubs are typically geared toward couple-swapping and group sex. The atmosphere is often that of a nightclub, with a dance floor, a social bar area, and designated playrooms. BDSM Dungeons are specifically designed for kinky play. The focus is on power exchange and scene dynamics.

- **Navigating the Space:** When you arrive, your first job is to get the lay of the land. Identify the social areas, play areas, and the restrooms. Most importantly, identify the safety monitors (often called Dungeon Masters or DMs). They are your first point of contact if you see a problem, feel unsafe, or have a question about equipment.

- **Common Issue: The "Sunk Cost" Trap:** You paid a large entry fee. Now what? The consumer script in your head starts screaming, "I have to get my money's worth!" This is a dangerous trap.

The price of admission buys you one thing and one thing only: **access to the venue.** It does not buy you a hookup. It does not guarantee anyone will be interested in you. It does not entitle you to anyone's time or body. And it certainly does not obligate you to do anything you don't enthusiastically want to do. Your body and your consent are not for sale. Your autonomy is worth more than any ticket price.

Multi-Day Events: The Immersion Experience

Immersive, multi-day events are a whole other level of intensity and require significant planning.

- **The All-Inclusive Getaway (Resorts/Festivals):** These are high-energy, curated vacations. Pacing is everything. Manage your social energy, substance use, and sleep to avoid burnout. It is a marathon, not a sprint.

- **The Rustic Retreat (Camping/Communal Gatherings):** These have a "communal effort" vibe. You are a participant building a temporary village, not a consumer being entertained.

- **Self-Sufficiency is Non-Negotiable:** You are responsible for your own survival (food, water, shelter).

- **Radical Self-Reliance and its Limits:** This isn't about rugged individualism; it's about being a responsible member of a temporary village. Come prepared to care for yourself, but be ready to help your neighbor.

- **Vetting is Paramount:** In any multi-day event your safety depends on the competence of the organizers. Do your research. Do they have a long-standing positive reputation and a clear, enforced policy for handling consent violations? Do they have medical and mental health support on site? If you can't find clear answers to these questions, do not go.

NO-BULLSHIT TL;DR

- A safe space is a collective creation. Your primary job in any social setting is to be a good bystander and contribute to a culture of consent.

- The rules apply to everyone, especially the host. A host who breaks their own rules is not safe. Your body is never the price of admission.

- If you are a guest, be a co-creator, not just a consumer. Respect the host, contribute to the space, and take full responsibility for anyone you bring with you.

- Trust your gut. If you feel unsafe or realize you were invited under false pretenses, it is always okay to leave. Your autonomy is worth more than any ticket price.

CHAPTER 24: SEX

DESIRES, RISKS, & REAL TALK

Let's be real: you probably didn't pick up this book to become more celibate. If you're practicing Ethical Non-Monogamy, sex is a central part of the conversation. It is a powerful force for intimacy, pleasure, and connection. Yet the way people talk about it in ENM often falls into one of two unhelpful camps: a fearful over-focus on risk that sterilize the joy, or a breezy "anything goes" attitude that glosses over the real complexities of consent, desire, and safety.

The goal is to engage with sex in a way that is clear-eyed, responsible, and pleasure-focused. It's about how to have amazing, consensual, and joyful sex without losing your damn mind—or compromising your health.

THE FOUNDATIONAL CONVERSATIONS

Before you can have amazing, consensual, and joyful sex without compromising your health or your relationships, you have to talk about it. These are the foundational conversations that must happen before you ever step into a play space or go on a date.

First, Define "Sex"—For Yourself, Then with Your Partners

Before you can have a single conversation about agreements, you must tackle an inherited script that is a breeding ground for betrayal: the assumption that you and your partner(s) even mean the same thing when you use the word "sex."

Step 1: The Personal Inventory (The "For Yourself" Part)

Before you talk to anyone else, you have to get clear with yourself. This is a non-negotiable first step. Take out a piece of paper and ask yourself:

- What specific acts feel like "sex" to me?
- Which activities feel purely physical, and which ones create a deep sense of emotional bonding for me?
- Where are my personal boundaries? What is a "Hell Yes," a "Maybe," and a "Hell No"?

Get granular. Is it manual stimulation? Oral sex? Genital contact? Anal sex? Kissing? Cuddling after? Knowing your own internal map is the prerequisite for being able to share it with someone else.

Step 2: The Shared Blueprint (The "With Your Partners" Part)

Now that you have your own map, it's time to sit down with your partner and compare notes. This is not about one person dictating terms. It is about co-creating a shared blueprint. The goal is to get so ridiculously specific that there is no room for misunderstanding.

A great way to structure this conversation is to create a Yes/No/Maybe List together. You can use a simple chart:

Table 24.1: The Yes/No/Maybe Agreement Blueprint

Activity	My Feeling	Your Feeling	Our Agreement for Now
Kissing on a first date	Yes	Yes	Yes
Manual stimulation (giving/receiving)	Yes	No	No for now
Oral sex	Yes	Maybe	Let's discuss before it happens
Penile-vaginal intercourse	No	No	Hard No
Cuddling after play	Yes	Yes	Yes

This is not a one-time conversation. It is a living document. You can and should revisit it regularly, especially as you both gain more experience, and your comfort levels evolve. Having this tangible, co-created document is one of the most powerful tools you can have. It replaces vague assumptions with radical clarity.

Consent Isn't Just "Yes" or "No": It's F.R.I.E.S

Consent isn't a one-time checkbox; it's an ongoing process. The F.R.I.E.S. model, a framework popularized by Planned

Parenthood, is a powerful guide to ensure consent is genuine. It must be:

F - Freely given: It cannot be the result of pressure, guilt, or manipulation.

R - Reversible: You can change your mind at any point, for any reason.

I - Informed: You can't consent if you've been lied to or had critical information withheld.

E - Enthusiastic: It should be a "Hell yes!", not the absence of a "no."

S - Specific: Saying yes to one thing does not mean you've said yes to another. Consent to kiss is not consent to have oral sex. Consent for a hand on your thigh is not consent to be fingered. Consent must be sought and given at every step. A partner who respects you will honor a changed mind instantly. A partner who pouts, pressures, or acts offended is showing you they are not safe.

NO, YOU DON'T OWE ANYONE SEX. EVER

This is one of the most important lessons you will ever learn. The pressure to "be cool" or to not "ruin the vibe" can be immense. This is a powerful social script designed to keep people, especially women, compliant. You must build an iron-clad internal permission structure to honor your own boundaries, no matter the social context. Their emotional reaction to your boundary—whether it's disappointment, anger, or pouting—is their responsibility, not yours. Your safety is more important than their comfort. Your autonomy is more important than their party.

Practicing Your "No": Building the Muscle of Consent

Knowing you have the right to say "no" is one thing. Actually saying it in a charged moment, when you don't want to hurt someone's feelings or "ruin the vibe," is another. This is not an intellectual exercise; it is a physical skill that requires practice.

The No-Bullshit Exercise: Practice saying no out loud, by yourself, in a low-stakes environment. Stand in front of a mirror and say the words.

"No, I'm not comfortable with that."

"I'm going to stop you there."

"I'm enjoying this, but I'm not ready to go further."

"Let's pause for a minute."

It will feel awkward. That's the point. Building the muscle memory in a calm moment makes the words easier to find when your heart is pounding and your brain is fuzzy.

RISK MANAGEMENT: HEALTH & SAFETY

Safer Sex: The Non-Negotiable Foundation

Sexually transmitted infections (STIs) are a normal, manageable reality of being a sexually active human being. They are not a moral failing or a sign that someone is "dirty." You must replace fear and shame with education and communication.

Let's be real: this conversation can feel awkward as hell, especially if it's new to you. That's okay. Pushing through a moment of awkwardness to ensure everyone can make informed, consensual decisions is one of the most profound acts of care you can offer a partner.

There is no such thing as 100% "safe sex," only informed, consensual risk.

A Note for the "Out of Practice": Always Be Prepared

If you are coming out of a long-term monogamous relationship, the entire landscape of safer sex may feel new or overwhelming. You might not have had to think about carrying condoms in twenty years. You might not be expecting a fun, casual date to escalate, and so you arrive unprepared—both for the conversation and for the act itself.

This is a non-negotiable part of ethical practice: if there is any possibility of sexual contact, you must be prepared. This means:

1. **Physically Prepared:** Have safer sex supplies (condoms, dental dams, lube) with you. Do not assume they will have them. Taking responsibility for your own safety is a profound act of self-respect.

2. **Mentally Prepared:** Have the "safer sex talk" rehearsed in your mind. Be ready to ask about testing and to share your own status before things get heated.

3. **Plan for Arousal:** Your brain works differently when you're turned on. Plan ahead for this. Don't make it hard to get to your safer sex supplies. Keep them in an easily accessible place, not buried at the bottom of a bag in another room. The fewer barriers there are to practicing safer sex, the more likely you are to do it.

The "safer sex talk" is a non-negotiable part of this.

- **A Red Flag:** When you ask someone about their STI status, an answer like "I'm good" or "I'm clean" is not acceptable. It signals a lack of sexual health literacy or an unwillingness to be transparent.

- **A Green Flag:** A responsible person will be able to tell you when they were last tested, what they were tested for, and what their sexual activity (and barrier use) has been since that test.

A Clean Test is Not a Green Light for Unprotected Sex

A recent, clean STI test is necessary information for assessing risk, but it is not a green light to have unprotected sex. A test is a snapshot in time. It does not account for any sexual activity they have had since that test, nor does it account for the window period of certain STIs. The only time unprotected sex is a responsible option is within a formal, negotiated, and fully informed fluid-bonding agreement.

Fluid Bonding: The High-Trust, High-Stakes Agreement

Fluid bonding is the agreement between partners to stop using barrier methods. It is not a casual decision; it is a significant escalation of trust that requires a strict, non-negotiable protocol. Unilaterally violating this agreement is a profound betrayal and an act of potential endangerment.

Table 24.2: The Five-Step Fluid Bonding Protocol

Step	Action	Why It Matters
1. Testing	Both partners receive a comprehensive STI panel.	Establishes a clear baseline of health and risk.
2. Results Sharing	Partners openly share their full results with each other.	Builds trust, transparency, and informed decision-making.
3. Disclosure Window	Partners agree on a time window (e.g., 30-60 days) of no new sexual activity with others before bonding.	Ensures no recent exposures compromise the decision.
4. Agreement Setting	Partners discuss and document agreements (e.g., exclusivity, regular testing frequency, changes protocol).	Clarifies expectations, boundaries, and accountability.
5. Ongoing Maintenance	Continued testing, communication, and review of agreements over time.	Maintains safety and respect long-term.

THE HARD LINE ON DRUGS & DECEPTION

Your safety, and the safety of the entire community, depends on absolute clarity around substances.

Do Not Give People Drugs. Period. This is not a "gift" or a way to "help someone loosen up." Giving someone a substance—even alcohol—without their full, informed consent is a form of assault.

Deception When Offering is a Firing Offense. Offering someone a sip of your drink without telling them it contains alcohol is a grievous breach of trust. Just because they backpedaled into "asking consent" after crossing your boundary does not make it okay, and you don't have to pretend otherwise.

NAVIGATING IN-THE-MOMENT SCENARIOS

The Internal Monologue of Ethical Sex: A Gut-Check Before You Act

Learning to recognize your own internal monologue is a superpower. If you find yourself having any of the following thoughts, it is a sign to STOP, pause, and reconsider your actions.

- **The Repeated Ask:** Thinking, "Maybe if I ask one more time, in a different way, they'll say yes," after they have already said no–STOP. You are no longer inviting; you are pressuring.

- **The "Impaired Opportunity":** Thinking, "They're pretty drunk right now, this might be my only chance," –STOP. This is predatory thinking. Consent cannot be given by someone who is significantly impaired.

- **The "4 AM" Test:** If you are thinking of initiating a hookup at 4 AM, ask yourself: "Did we build the connection for this before it was 4 AM?" If you are approaching someone you just met who was passed out on a couch five minutes ago, STOP.

The Power of the Pause: Your Best Tool

The most powerful tool you have is the pause. You are always allowed to slow down. Anyone who pressures you to decide right now is showing you that your comfort is less important than their desire.

NO-BULLSHIT TL;DR

- Define your terms. Never assume "sex" means the same thing to everyone. Specificity is the foundation of consent.

- Consent is F.R.I.E.S.: Freely given, Reversible, Informed, Enthusiastic, and Specific. You never owe anyone sex, ever. Your safety is more important than their comfort.

- Safer sex is a non-negotiable practice of care. Replace shame with education, and demand open communication about testing and risk. A clean test is not a green light for unprotected sex.

- Listen to your internal monologue. If you find yourself trying to pressure, persuade, or take advantage of an opportunity, pause. Your integrity is on the line.

CHAPTER 25: MONEY, LAW, & PRACTICALITIES

THE UNSEXY STUFF THAT SAVES YOUR ASS

It's romantic to talk about love and thrilling to talk about sex. It is deeply, profoundly unsexy to talk about cohabitation agreements, healthcare proxies, and who is paying for the extra data on the family phone plan. This may be the least glamorous chapter in the book—and it might be the most important. This is the chapter about how you show up for your partners when the worst happens. It's about translating the beautiful ideals of love and commitment into the real-world, legally binding documents that protect your chosen family.

Ignoring the practical realities of non-monogamy is one of the fastest ways to turn a beautiful connection into a swamp of resentment and legal chaos. Our legal and financial systems are designed for the monogamous married couple. If you are creating a life outside that model, you are operating without automatic protections. You must build your own.

FINANCIAL ETHICS IN A POLYCULE

Money can be a stand-in for time, energy, and value. How it is handled in a relationship network speaks

volumes about the underlying ethics of that network.

Be Real About Income Disparities

It is rare for all partners in a polycule to have the same income. Pretending these differences don't exist is a fantasy. "Fair" does not always mean "equal." A partner who earns less may contribute in other valuable ways—household labor, logistical planning, emotional support. An ethical polycule values all forms of contribution, not just financial ones.

Value Time as a Currency

This is a huge blind spot in a world that has taught us to measure our worth by our income—a toxic inherited script. Your partner's time is not a commodity to be valued against your own. In our culture, we are taught to equate a person's value with their hourly wage. Do not bring this poisonous, transactional logic into your relationships. If you catch yourself thinking your time is inherently more valuable than a partner's because you earn more, that is a signal to stop and look at yourself.

Generosity is Not a Transaction

A gift is a gift. A transaction is a transaction. Paying for something does not buy you a "right" to someone else's time, affection, or body. The insidious "but I bought you dinner…"

logic isn't generosity; it's financial coercion. It's an attempt to turn a gift into a debt and a partner into an employee.

Keep Your Financial Agreements Clean

If a partner lends you fifty dollars, pay them back fifty dollars. Don't show up a week later with a "thoughtful" gift and say, "We're even now, right?" This is a profound sign of disrespect. It removes their agency to decide how their own money is spent.

LEGAL PROTECTIONS FOR YOUR CHOSEN FAMILY

The legal system grants automatic rights to married couples. In a polycule with non-married partners, you have none of these by default. You must create them yourselves by consulting a poly-friendly lawyer—and because family law varies dramatically by state and jurisdiction, it is essential that this attorney is **local**. **Do not wait for a crisis.** Here are the essential protections you need to build:

- **To Control Healthcare Decisions:** A Healthcare Proxy is a non-negotiable document. It gives a person you trust the legal authority to make medical decisions for you if you are incapacitated. Without it, that power could default to an estranged family member, potentially barring your partners from your hospital room.

- **To Protect Inheritance & Assets:** A Will or Living Trust is the only way to ensure your property goes to your chosen family. Without one, the state's default rules apply, meaning your unmarried partner of 20 years could be left with nothing while your assets go to a distant biological relative.

- **To Secure a Shared Home:** When you live together without being married, a Cohabitation Agreement is essential. It functions like a prenup, defining how shared property and finances will be handled if you break up, ensuring no one is left homeless or without their fair share.

- **To Solidify Parenthood:** For non-biological parents, a formal Parenting Agreement and, where legally available, a Second-Parent Adoption are crucial. These are the only ways to guarantee your rights to custody and visitation, protecting your relationship with a child you are raising. The laws governing parental rights are highly specific to your state or jurisdiction; consulting a local family law attorney is non-negotiable.

Case Study: The Hospital Door

Daniel and his nesting partner, Sasha, have been together for 15 years. Daniel also has a long-term partner, Michael. Daniel is in a serious car accident and is unconscious. Because they have no legal paperwork, the hospital only allows Daniel's estranged parents to see him and make medical decisions. Sasha and Michael are relegated to the waiting room, unable to advocate for the man they love.

NO-BULLSHIT TL;DR

- Money is a tool. Use it ethically. Be transparent about income differences and value all forms of contribution, not just financial ones.

- Do not bring the toxic script of the marketplace into your relationships. A person's worth is not their hourly wage.

- Generosity is a gift, not a transaction. You cannot use money to buy affection or obligate a partner.

- The legal system is not built for you. Proactive legal planning (wills, healthcare proxies) is not a sign of distrust; it is the ultimate act of protecting your chosen family.

CHAPTER 26: THE GEOGRAPHY OF LOVE

NAVIGATING LONG DISTANCE RELATIONSHIPS

In the ecosystem of Ethical Non-Monogamy, some of our most profound connections are not with the person we wake up next to every morning, but with a partner who lives a plane ride away. Navigating a long-distance relationship (LDR) is a challenge under any circumstances. Navigating multiple relationships, with one or more at a distance, is a masterclass in communication and resource management.

But the biggest challenge isn't the miles; it's the mindset. Distance creates a unique and dangerous relational dynamic: the potential for a relationship to exist in a permanent state of New Relationship Energy.

THE PERMA-NRE TRAP

Proximity is the cure for idealization. It forces you to deal with the messy realities of another human being. A long-distance relationship is often shielded from this. Your time together is a curated highlight reel, a vacation from normal life.

This creates a dangerous imbalance. The long-distance partner remains a perfect, idealized figure—a character from the romantic fairytale script we were all taught to crave. Meanwhile, your local partners are the ones navigating the everyday realities of your shared life, your stress, and your full humanity. This is the perma-NRE trap, and if left unexamined, it can slowly poison your entire relationship network.

The Binge and Purge Cycle of ENM

The perma-NRE trap leads directly to the most common failure mode of LDRs: the binge. When your long-distance partner visits, the temptation to spend every moment with them is immense. This is a recipe for disaster. You are not just having a reunion; you are effectively detonating your local life. Through your actions, you are telling your other partners that they are the mundane "real life" you need a vacation from, while your long-distance partner is the exciting escape. This is a catastrophic failure to manage the finite resources we discussed in Chapter 7, and it is a profound act of disrespect to the people who show up for you every day.

The Comet as a Practice: Pacing is a Form of Care

A comet is an LDR partner with whom one has a significant but infrequent connection. But a comet is more than just a person; it's a *practice*. It is the conscious art of pacing a relationship to preserve its energy without letting it destabilize your life. Ethical practice is often about deliberately pacing your time with people, especially when your NRE screams to do the opposite.

- **Communication Rituals:** Schedule video dates and treat them like real dates. Use asynchronous tools like voice notes to share thoughts without the pressure of an immediate response.

- **Building a Shared World:** Learn the names of their local friends and metamours. This makes their world feel real and connected to yours.

- **Integrate, Don't Compartmentalize:** Talk about your comet with your local partners (with everyone's consent, of course). This makes all relationships feel real and integrated, rather than creating a secret, fantasy world that exists in a separate compartment.

THE ETHICS OF TIMING: WHEN "NO" MEANS "NOT NOW"... AND WHEN IT JUST MEANS "NO"

Sometimes, the most profound ethical challenges are not about distance, but about timing. You might meet a person you have incredible chemistry with, but the timing is simply wrong (they might be polysaturated, in a crisis, or your best friend's new lover). In these moments, the most ethical thing you can do is often nothing at all. Rushing in to stake your claim is a move driven by scarcity and ego. Having the self-regulation to wait is a sign of immense integrity.

The No-Bullshit Reality Check: This requires you to navigate a very blurry line with a high degree of emotional intelligence.

1. **"Stepping Back" Can Be a Gift of Friendship:** You're at a party and you feel an intense spark with someone new. But then you learn that your close

friend, who is also there, has a massive, long-standing crush on that same person. This is a classic ethical test. The world of scarcity and the Monogamy Mindset would tell you to "stake your claim" before your friend does.

a. The ethical path, born from a mindset of abundance and deep respect for your friendships, is to consider **stepping back**.

b. This isn't about some juvenile concept of "dibs." It's a conscious, compassionate act of prioritizing a valued, long-term friendship over the intoxicating but fleeting rush of a new spark. It's a choice to not turn your friend into your romantic rival. An ethical response in this moment might be to quietly pull your friend aside and say: "Hey, I just want you to know, Sarah is amazing, but I know how much you like her. I'm going to step back and give you space. Your friendship means more to me than this." This is an act of profound integrity.

2. **"Not Now" Can Be a Polite "No.":** Let's be real: many people, especially women, are socialized to be polite rather than direct. They may say "not now" when they really mean "no, never." It is a sad reality that a hard "no" can sometimes provoke a dangerous reaction, so a soft "no" is used as a de-escalation tactic.

3. **Don't be a Bulldozer:** Your job is to listen for the truth underneath the words. If you ask someone out

and they say, "not now," the respectful move is to accept that answer and move on. Don't ask them again every time you see them. Turning their polite rejection into a recurring negotiation is a form of harassment. It ignores their "no" and centers your own desire.

The Litmus Test: The ethical path is to treat every "no" as a "no forever," unless the other person explicitly and enthusiastically invites you to revisit the conversation later. The burden is on them to re-open the door, not on you to keep knocking on it.

NO-BULLSHIT TL;DR

- Beware the "perma-NRE" trap. Proximity is the cure for idealization. Work actively to see your long-distance partner as a whole, flawed human, not a fantasy.

- Do not binge on a partner when they visit. Honoring your commitments to your local partners, even when it's hard, is an act of profound integrity.

- The ethics of timing are crucial. Respect a "not now," and understand that it might be a polite "no." Do not be the person who keeps asking.

- The goal is to integrate your LDR into your life, not use it as a vacation from your life.

CHAPTER 27: POLYAMORY & PARENTHOOD

THE PRIMARY DIRECTIVE: PROTECTING YOUR KIDS IN A COMPLEX WORLD

It's one thing to talk about polyamory when you're single and child-free. It's another thing entirely when you're coordinating custody schedules with an ex who is convinced you've joined a sex cult, while trying to explain to your six-year-old why your "special friend" Taylor sometimes sleeps over.

This is where the lofty ideals of relational freedom meet the messy reality of family life.

THE PRIMARY DIRECTIVE: THE CHILD'S WELL-BEING COMES FIRST

Let's establish the one non-negotiable principle: The child's need for safety, stability, and security is not just a filter for your decisions; it is the unshakeable priority.

Your needs are valid. Your desire for a hot new date, the intoxicating pull of NRE, and your fundamental need for adult time are all real and important. And... they all come second. Full stop. This doesn't mean you stop being a whole person. It means you have accepted the profound responsibility of parenthood, and that responsibility now defines the ethical container in which your non-monogamy can exist.

THE PARENT'S PARADOX: NAVIGATING YOUR NEEDS & THEIRS

Dismantling the "Choosing Me" Bullshit

There is a particularly toxic strain of self-help culture that has seeped into ENM spaces: the "I am choosing myself" self-actualization trap. Your choices have a profound impact on your kids. To pretend otherwise is not enlightened; it's a cowardly abdication of your responsibility. There are times of profound hardship where you must focus on yourself to survive, but using "self-love" as a perpetual excuse to de-prioritize your children is not the way.

From Guilt to Action: The Work of a Good Parent

Feeling guilty about your past mistakes does not make you a bad parent. It is proof that you are a good one.

The fact that you feel guilt means you have a conscience. The person who doesn't look back and recognize their impact on others is the person to worry about. The trap is not the feeling of guilt; it's becoming paralyzed by it, stuck in a loop of shame about the past. The work of a good parent—and the core work of this book—is to turn that reflection into repair. It's about taking the wisdom from past missteps and using it to make a more conscious choice in the present. The hard question isn't just "What did I do wrong?" but "What can I do now to repair and be the parent my child needs today?"

Parenting in Practice: The Long Game

The investment of your time and presence now has an exponentially bigger payoff in their future. What might seem like a small thing to you—a missed bedtime story, being emotionally checked out for a week because of NRE—can have a massive impact on a child. A dinner with a new date might be fun for a night; missing your kid's school play is a memory that sticks. The most important way to teach your children ethics is by your example.

THE PARTNER INTRODUCTION PROTOCOL: A STEP-BY-STEP GUIDE

Introducing a new partner to your child is a major step. This protocol is your shield to protect your child's heart. When in doubt, always wait longer. Your primary job is to protect your child from the chaos of a revolving door of partners.

- **Stage 1: Pre-Introduction Self-Audit.** Is this relationship stable? Are we out of the intense NRE phase? Does this person respect my role as a parent? What is our plan if we break up?

- **Stage 2: The First Meeting.** Talk to your child first using a low-pressure label like "my friend." The first meeting should be in a neutral, low-stakes environment like a park.

- **Stage 3: Ongoing Integration.** Let your child set the pace. Involve the new partner in casual group activities before inviting them into more intimate home settings.

NAVIGATING THE REAL WORLD

Strategic Disclosure: A Risk/Benefit Analysis

You do not owe your child's teacher a PowerPoint presentation on your relationship structure. Your family's privacy is a valid boundary. You need to make a conscious risk/benefit analysis for your specific situation, considering legal, social, and family risks.

CO-PARENTING WITH A HOSTILE EX

This is one of the most challenging scenarios in non-monogamy. When co-parenting with an ex who disapproves of your lifestyle, your best tools are not arguments but actions. Your primary strategy must be de-escalation.

You cannot win a fight with someone who is determined to misunderstand you, but you can refuse to participate in it. The most powerful tool for this is the **BIFF** method, a framework developed by conflict resolution expert Bill Eddy. The goal is to keep all written communication **B**rief, **I**nformative, **F**riendly, and **F**irm. It's a strategy designed to shut down conflict by giving it no emotional fuel. Your only job is to communicate necessary information.

Let's see it in action. Imagine you receive this email from your ex:

I can't believe what I'm hearing about your "lifestyle." I don't want all these random people around our kids. It's unstable, and frankly, I'm considering talking to my lawyer about custody. You need to get your priorities straight. By the way, what time are you picking up the kids on Friday?

A reactive, defensive response would be a page-long justification of your life. A BIFF response looks like this:

Hi [Ex's Name],

I'll be there to pick up the kids at 5 p.m. on Friday. Hope you have a good week.

Best, [Your Name]

Notice what this response does not do. It does not defend. It does not apologize. It does not engage with a single accusation. It is **brief** (two sentences), **informative** (answers the only logistical question), **friendly** (a neutral pleasantry), and **firm** (refuses to be drawn into the drama). It starves the conflict of oxygen. In the face of their attempts to question your stability, you prove it by being the most boringly responsible parent on the planet.

Your Children as a Litmus Test for New Partners

Your parenting responsibilities are not weeds choking your garden; they are the deep, rich soil that your garden grows in and is anchored by. They are the source of its greatest strength.

Anyone who sees your children as an inconvenience—as something to be worked around rather than nurtured—is not just a bad fit for your polycule. They are poison to your soil. They are the wrong partner for you.

NO-BULLSHIT TL;DR

- Your child's need for safety and stability is your unshakeable priority. This is the ethical container for your non-monogamy.

- Your choices have a profound impact. The "I'm choosing me" self-help script does not absolve you of your responsibility as a parent.

- Parental guilt is not a sign that you are a bad parent; it's a sign that you are a good one with a conscience. The work is turning that guilt into responsible action today.

- Introduce new partners to your children slowly, carefully, and only when the relationship is stable. Protect them from chaos.

PART 5: THE LIGHT & DARK SIDES

CHAPTER 28: THE SINGLE MAN

A GUIDE TO NAVIGATING DOUBLE STANDARDS & NOT BEING A CLICHÉ

In the ecosystem of Ethical Non-Monogamy, there is perhaps no figure more stereotyped or viewed with more automatic suspicion than the single, heterosexual man. He is often seen as a predator, a tourist, a threat, or, at best, a convenient accessory. While these stereotypes are often rooted in legitimate bad experiences, they create a landscape where even the most ethical and well-intentioned single man is often treated as guilty until proven innocent.

This is a guide for the ethically minded single man trying to navigate a world that is often wary of him. More importantly, it is a call to awareness for the partnered people who, often unconsciously, perpetuate a toxic double standard.

THE LANDSCAPE OF ASSUMPTIONS

A single man entering an ENM space, particularly a couple-centric one, walks into a minefield of pre-existing assumptions.

These are often the ghosts of the Monogamy Mindset, where any man not in a committed couple is automatically viewed with suspicion, a script that still runs in the background even in "liberated" spaces. He is often stereotyped as:

- **A Player in Disguise:** Using "ENM" to get laid without commitment.

- **A Cowboy:** Secretly trying to "rope off" a woman from her existing relationship.

- **A Threat:** His very presence is seen as a direct threat to the stability of existing couples.

- **A Prop:** He may be seen as a "bull" or a "stud"–a tool for a couple's pleasure, not a person. This is the world where you will hear the dehumanizing phrase, "dicks are a dime a dozen."

THE DOUBLE STANDARD OF CONSEQUENCES

This landscape of assumptions creates a brutal double standard. A single man can make the exact same mistake as a partnered man and face a profoundly different consequence.

Imagine a communication misstep: a partner is clumsy with their words or fumbles an agreement.

- When a partnered man makes this mistake, it's often seen as a symptom–"He's stressed at work"–and a problem to be solved within the relationship.

- When a single man makes the exact same mistake, it is often seen as evidence: proof of his fundamental character flaws. He has little to no relational equity to fall back on. His mistake is a data point proving he is a bad investment, and he is often summarily dismissed.

The bar for grace is set much lower.

THE GRATITUDE TRAP: THE PRESSURE TO NOT SAY NO

This power imbalance creates another insidious dynamic: the pressure for the single man to be grateful for any attention he receives. Because he is often seen as being of low value, there's an unspoken expectation that he should be happy to get whatever he can.

This puts immense pressure on him to not say "no" to a social invitation or a sexual overture. This undermines his autonomy and his right to have his own preferences. This is the core of objectification: the belief that someone exists for your use and should be thankful for the opportunity. Refusing to participate in this dynamic—by holding your boundaries and unapologetically having your own preferences— is not just an act of self-respect. It is an act of service to the entire community, as it helps to dismantle a toxic, inherited power imbalance.

A NO-BULLSHIT GUIDE TO NAVIGATING WITH INTEGRITY

If you are a single man in ENM, your task is not to be defensive but to operate with such impeccable integrity that you actively defy the clichés. This isn't about being "Good Enough" to be accepted; it's about being so grounded in your own ethics that you become a force for positive change in the community.

- **Be an Impeccable Communicator:** Be ruthlessly clear and reliable. Confirm dates. Show up on time. State your intentions honestly. In a world that assumes you're a flake; your reliability is your greatest asset.

- **Show You've Done the Work:** Signal your investment in ethical practice. Mentioning books you've read or concepts you're working with shows you're not a tourist; you're a resident.

- **Vet Your Partners Ruthlessly:** Do not fall into the gratitude trap. You have the right to choose your partners just as much as they have the right to choose you. If a couple's answers reveal they see you as a prop, walk away.

- **Hold Your Boundaries Firmly:** You are allowed to say no. A couple or partner who respects you will see this as a green flag. One who sees it as an inconvenience is telling you everything you need to know about how they value you.

A GUIDE FOR THOSE DATING SINGLE MEN: A CALL FOR ETHICAL ENGAGEMENT

If you are a couple or a partnered person, you have a profound responsibility to treat the single men you date with dignity.

- **Treat Them as Whole People:** He is not a "stud," a "bull," or a "third." He is a human being with his own needs, desires, and emotional life.

- **Be Radically Honest About Your Intentions:** Be upfront about the level of commitment and integration you are truly offering. Do not lead someone on with a vague promise of "seeing where things go."

- **Share the Labor:** The emotional and logistical labor of scheduling should not fall solely on the "flexible" single person.

- **Dismantle Your Couple Privilege:** Do not treat him as a guest in your relationship. His needs and feelings are just as valid as yours.

NO-BULLSHIT TL;DR

- Single men in ENM often face a double standard where their mistakes are treated as evidence of character flaws, not as simple human errors.

- Beware the "Gratitude Trap"—the unspoken pressure to accept any offer and have no needs of your own. Your autonomy is not negotiable.

- The path forward is radical integrity. Be an impeccable communicator, hold your boundaries firmly, and ruthlessly vet partners who see you as a prop, not a person.

- For those who date single men: He is a whole person, not a disposable commodity. Dismantle your own couple privilege and treat his agency as equal to your own.

CHAPTER 29: THE SINGLE WOMAN

A GUIDE TO NAVIGATING THE PEDESTAL & DODGING UNICORN HUNTERS

In the world of Ethical Non-Monogamy, the single woman is often placed on a pedestal, only to find that the pedestal is a cage. She is simultaneously idealized and objectified, sought after and stereotyped. She is the mythical "Unicorn," the "Free Spirit," the "Cool Girl" who is expected to be beautiful, bisexual, and blessedly free of drama.

This is a guide for the single woman navigating a landscape that often wants to put her in a box. More importantly, it is a call to awareness for the partnered people who project these fantasies onto single women.

THE PEDESTAL IS A CAGE: THE PARADOX OF COMMODITY

Unlike the single man who is often treated as a low-value commodity, the single woman is frequently treated as a high-value one. This is not a privilege; it is the same patriarchal script that has always defined a woman's worth by her desirability to men, just given a progressive ENM spin. It is a different flavor of dehumanization. Being seen as a desirable "object" means you are inundated with attention, but much of it is low-effort and centered on what you can provide rather than who you are.

People aren't connecting with you; they are connecting with the idea of you. You become a screen onto which they project their fantasies, expecting you to play one of these impossible roles:

- **The Unicorn:** The ultimate fantasy object—a bisexual woman who will date a couple, be equally attracted to both, have no needs of her own that might inconvenience the primary relationship, and magically solve all their intimacy problems. She is not a person; she is a perfect, living sex toy.

- **The Cool Girl:** The woman who is "not like the others." She's expected to be endlessly accommodating, never jealous, and require zero emotional labor.

- **The Emotional Fixer:** A couple, often new to ENM, will seek out an experienced single woman with the unspoken expectation that she will do the heavy lifting of managing their transition and teaching them how to "do poly." You are not a partner; you are a consultant they are trying to fuck.

- **The Homewrecker:** The moment the "Cool Girl" or "Unicorn" shows she has her own needs or boundaries, the fantasy shatters. The pedestal is kicked out from under her, and she is swiftly recast as a "Threat" or "Drama Queen."

THE INTERNALIZED PRESSURE: THE IMPOSSIBLE DOUBLE-BIND

This constant external pressure often creates an internal one. It's the trap of trying to be the fantasy, of silencing your own needs to avoid "causing trouble." For women, this is compounded by a lifetime of contradictory social conditioning:

> You are taught your entire life not to be a "whore," but in ENM spaces, you can be shamed for not being "open" enough.

This is a specific and manipulative trap. The very presence of a single woman in a lifestyle space is sometimes treated as assumed consent—the idea that by simply being there, you are available to everyone. This is bullshit. It is a predatory tactic that uses the language of liberation to shame you into compliance. Your "no" is not just a personal boundary; it is a radical act of rebellion against a script that wants to treat you as a public utility. It is a sacred act of self-respect.

RECLAIMING THE "UNICORN": WHEN BEING THE THIRD IS THE GOAL

After all these warnings, it would be easy to conclude that any couple seeking a third person is predatory. That is not the full truth. While unicorn hunting is a real and harmful practice, it is a profound mistake to dismiss the agency of the many solo people who actively and joyfully seek out connections with couples.

For them, being a "third" is not a sign of being used; it is their ideal relationship dynamic. The appeal is often:

- **Low Entanglement:** They can enjoy deep sexual and social connection without the pressures of merging lives or climbing the relationship escalator.

- **Fulfilling a Fantasy:** The dynamic of a threesome is an exciting and valid desire.

- **Shared Connection:** Some people find deep satisfaction and arousal in being invited into the intimate space of a loving couple, witnessing and contributing to their bond.

The No-Bullshit Difference: The problem is never the structure of a triad. The problem is objectification. The work, then, is not to avoid couples, but to become an expert at differentiating between predatory Unicorn Hunters and ethical Partners.

Table 29.1: The Litmus Test: Hunters vs. Partners

Unicorn Hunters (The Red Flag)	Ethical Partners (The Green Flag)
They are looking for a "third" to "complete" them or "fit into" their lives.	They are looking for a "person" to "connect with" and "build something new" with.
They have a list of pre-written rules for you to follow.	They want to co-create agreements with you that honor everyone's needs.
They expect you to be equally attracted to both of them, instantly.	They respect that attraction is complex and allow connections to form organically.
They get defensive if you have your own boundaries or needs.	They celebrate your autonomy and see your boundaries as a sign of health.

Your desire to connect with couples is valid. Your job is to wield your agency with power and to accept nothing less than being treated as a whole, desired, and respected partner in the experience.

A NO-BULLSHIT GUIDE TO NAVIGATING WITH POWER & INTEGRITY

Your primary task is to hold fiercely to your own autonomy, trust your instincts, and develop a ruthless vetting process that filters for partners who see you as a whole person, not a fantasy.

Practice Saying "No"

You are your own primary advocate. Practice saying "no" clearly, kindly, and without apology.

"No, thank you."

"I'm not feeling it, but I appreciate the offer."

"That's not something I'm interested in, but I hope you have a great night."

A person who respects you will accept your "no" with grace. A person who argues or pouts is showing you that your comfort is less important than their ego.

Your Profile Is a Bouncer, Not a Welcome Mat

Your dating profile is a filter designed to keep out the timewasters. Be unapologetically clear about who you are and what you want.

"I am a solo polyamorous woman looking for a deep, committed partnership. I do not date established couples."

"I enjoy casual connections and am open to dating individuals and ethically minded couples who treat me as an equal partner, not an accessory."

"I will not be your teacher, your therapist, or the 'fix' for your relationship. Come to me whole, having done your own work."

"My autonomy is my first priority. I am not interested in hierarchical relationships where I would be subject to a veto."

This will scare off the people you don't want to date anyway. Good. That's its job.

- THE VETTING PROCESS: A GUIDE TO SPOTTING THE BULLSHIT

When you connect with a couple, be a ruthless detective. Your job is to gather data. The following questions are designed to reveal their underlying philosophy: do they see you as a whole person or a convenient accessory? Listen carefully not just to what they say, but how they say it.

- Ask: "How are your agreements structured for a new person joining you?"

- Green Flag: They talk about their *internal* agreements as tools for their own alignment but emphasize that any new relationship will require co-creating new agreements that respect everyone. They are excited by this prospect.

230

- Yellow Flag: They say, "We have a few basic rules, but we're open to discussing them." This is a sign to get curious. It could mean they are new and haven't thought it through, or it could be a soft "no" in disguise. Your follow-up is: "I'd love to hear what they are. Which of those are you genuinely flexible on?"

- Red Flag: They present you with a pre-written, non-negotiable list of "rules" for you to follow. This tells you that you are an accessory entering their structure, not a partner helping to build a new one.

- Ask: "What emotional labor do you expect from a new partner in navigating your dynamic?"

- Green Flag: "None. Our emotional work is our own. Our baggage is our own to carry. We're looking for a partner, not a therapist."

- Yellow Flag: They hesitate or say something vague like, "Well, we just hope everyone can be mature and communicate." This isn't a deal-breaker, but it's a sign they may not have fully considered this. Your follow-up is: "What does that look like in practice when one of you is having a hard time?"

- Red Flag: Any language that hints at you helping one partner "get more comfortable" or "feel more secure." This is a giant warning sign that you are being interviewed for an unpaid emotional caretaking job.

- Ask: "Do either of you have veto power over the other's relationships?"

- Green Flag: "Absolutely not. We don't believe in having that kind of power over each other's relationships. We trust each other to manage our own connections."

- Yellow Flag: They say something like, "We have one in case of emergency, but we've never used it." This requires deep investigation. It may be a relic from their early, insecure days, or it may be a gun they are fully prepared to use on you. Your follow-up is: "Can you walk me through a scenario where you imagine using it?"

- Red Flag: "Yes, we have a veto to keep our primary relationship safe." This is the biggest red flag of all. It means your relationship has a built-in kill switch that you don't control. You are, by definition, disposable.

A NOTE TO COUPLES: HOW NOT TO BE A UNICORN HUNTER

If you are a couple reading this, listen up. The antidote to unicorn hunting is not to forbid dating as a couple; many people—including the "unicorns" themselves—actively seek out and enjoy this dynamic.

The antidote is to **dismantle the hierarchy in your own minds.** It requires a profound shift from asking, "How can we find someone to fit into *our* relationship?" to asking, "What new, beautiful relationship can the *three of us* build together as equals?"

This means you don't present a new person with a pre-written rulebook; you co-create your agreements together. It means you see their needs, fears, and desires as being just as valid as your own. It means you are not looking for an accessory to your coupledom, but a whole person to build a new connection with. A triad is not something you find; it is something that might, with a great deal of luck and ethical care, be built by three people, not two.

NO-BULLSHIT TL;DR

- Being placed on a pedestal is not a compliment; it is a cage. Being highly sought after is not the same as being highly valued.

- Your "no" is not a negotiation, a suggestion, or a moral failing. It is your sovereign right and a sacred act of self-respect.

- Use your dating profile as a bouncer, not a welcome mat. Be unapologetically clear about who you are and what you will and will not accept.

- Vet ruthlessly. Differentiate between ethical partners who want to connect with you, and unicorn hunters who want to consume a fantasy.

- You are the main character of your own story, not an accessory in someone else's.

CHAPTER 30: ENM IN THE SECOND HALF

NAVIGATING AGEISM, INEXPERIENCE, & THE "SECOND ADOLESCENCE"

When people picture Ethical Non-Monogamy, they often imagine a scene filled with young, urban, unencumbered individuals. But love, curiosity, and the desire for authentic connection have no age limit. A growing number of people are discovering ENM in their 50s, 60s, and beyond, and they bring with them a lifetime of experience, wisdom, and a unique set of challenges and superpowers.

STARTING LATER: THE GREAT UNLEARNING

Many people come to ENM in later life after decades in a monogamous marriage. This often happens after a divorce, the death of a spouse, or the realization that the old model no longer fits. This journey of "unlearning" comes with its own emotional hurdles. After decades of living by one set of rules, you are not just learning a new skill; you are dismantling the deepest inherited script of your life.

Discovering you are non-monogamous later in life can feel like a **second adolescence**: the thrill of a first kiss at fifty-five, the awkwardness of navigating dating apps, and the destabilizing but exhilarating feeling of realizing the old rules no longer apply. Giving yourself permission to be a beginner is crucial. Admitting you don't know everything, especially when you're older, is a sign of immense strength and self-awareness.

NAVIGATING AGEISM & EXPERIENCE

The dating and community landscape can look different for older adults. You will encounter ageism, and it cuts both ways.

- **You May Be Age-Shamed.** Younger people might dismiss you as being out of touch or "too old" for the scene. Conversely, you may find yourself less attracted to younger partners. You are allowed to have your preferences without being shamed for them. The work is to understand your own biases and remain open, but you do not owe anyone your attraction.

- **Do Not Weaponize Your Age.** On the flip side, do not assume that because you are older, you know how ENM works better than someone younger. Your decades in a monogamous marriage do not automatically translate to expertise in non-monogamy. Humility is your greatest asset.

TRAPS TO WATCH OUT FOR

The "Making Up for Lost Time" Wrecking Ball

This is one of the most common traps for those starting later. You may have come from a restrictive background and now feel an intense urge to make up for lost time. This can lead to a frantic, NRE-fueled chaos where you move too quickly and leave a trail of hurt feelings. This impulse is born from joy, not malice—the exhilarating feeling of a door swinging open after a lifetime in a closed room. Your newfound freedom is valid, but it is not a license to be reckless with other people's hearts. The work is to temper that joy with the wisdom and care your life experience has given you.

Feigning Ignorance

You genuinely might have grown up in a different time. The language and social norms of modern ENM might be completely new. That's okay. What is not okay is feigning ignorance to excuse bad behavior. "I didn't know that was a boundary" is a cowardly way to avoid accountability after you've caused harm. The ethical way to handle this is with proactive curiosity: "I'm new to this, and I know the norms are different. If I ever misstep, please tell me. I am here to learn."

THE SUPERPOWER OF LIVED EXPERIENCE

Your life experience is a superpower. You have likely navigated marriages, divorces, careers, and raising children. You know who you are and what you will not tolerate. You have a depth of emotional resilience that many younger people are still developing. Your perspective is incredibly helpful to the community. In a scene that can sometimes be swept up in the drama of youthful NRE, you are the grounding force. You can be a mentor, a source of stability, and a living testament that authentic love is a lifelong journey.

NAVIGATING FAMILY DYNAMICS

One of the most significant challenges is navigating relationships with adult children, who may struggle with your new identity. They knew a different "you" for decades and may fear for your well-being or worry about inheritance. They may not approve. Visits with grandchildren may be discontinued. They are within their rights, just as you are to choose new partners.

Case Study: When Adult Children React

Meg and Dan, after a decade in the lifestyle, formed a triad with their partner, Dean. Before moving in together, they told their adult children. One daughter embraced their happiness. The other did not. Citing her own moral compass, she informed them they would never host their grandchildren at their home again and that her family would not attend any function that Dean also attended. This created a painful and lasting rift. The most effective strategy for Meg and Dan was to lead with confidence in their own choices, consistently reassure both daughters of their love, and give the disapproving daughter the space to process, without sacrificing the integrity of their own lives.

HEALTH & LONG-TERM CARE

In the second half of life, planning for retirement and potential health challenges becomes a more pressing reality. This is more complex with multiple, non-legal partners. Proactive legal and financial planning is absolutely essential. It's crucial to have explicit conversations about caregiving roles and to create a "care web" of partners and friends.

NO-BULLSHIT TL;DR

- Discovering ENM later in life is a valid path. Grant yourself the grace to be a beginner again.

- You will face ageism, and you have your own biases to unlearn. Do not weaponize your age or your experience; lead with humility.

- Beware the "making up for lost time" trap. Your exhilarating freedom does not absolve you of your responsibility to treat others with care.

- Your lived experience is a superpower. Find the communities that value your wisdom and be the grounding force they need.

- Navigating family dynamics requires confidence, compassion, and firm boundaries. Be prepared for complex conversations.

CHAPTER 31: NAVIGATING CHRONIC ILLNESS & DISABILITY

A GUIDE TO ACCESS INTIMACY, INTERDEPENDENT CARE, & RADICAL HONESTY

In the able-bodied and neurotypical world, we are taught to see capacity as a stable, renewable resource. We assume a good night's sleep is enough to recharge and that our bodies will generally do what we ask. For people living with chronic illness, disability, or neurodivergence, this is a fantasy. And if you are one of the lucky ones for whom it is not a fantasy, this chapter is a demand that you see and care for the people in your community for whom it is.

And let's be devastatingly clear: many of these illnesses are invisible. People in our communities are navigating profound daily battles with depression, PTSD, anxiety, autoimmune disorders, and chronic pain that you cannot see. Sometimes, these are the most loving people in the room, precisely because they truly understand pain and empathy.

But this reality creates a profound tension within ENM spaces. When a community is framed as "fun" or a place to escape the "real world," it can create immense pressure to perform wellness. People with invisible illnesses often feel like they can't bring their full selves to the table because that means "bringing the vibe down."

This chapter is a call for a more honest and compassionate community, a guide for those who are suffering and for those who love them.

SPOON THEORY: THE LANGUAGE OF FINITE ENERGY

To understand disability in ENM, you must first understand **spoon theory**. Coined by Christine Miserandino, it's a metaphor for the finite energy a person has for daily activities. An able-bodied person might start the day with a seemingly unlimited supply of "spoons." A person with a chronic illness might start with only twelve. Getting out of bed costs a spoon. A deep, emotional conversation costs three. Once the spoons are gone, they are gone. There is no "pushing through."

A partner with a disability is not being "flaky" when they cancel plans; they are managing a budget of spoons that you may not be able to see.

THE "FUN VIBE" TRAP & ITS HIGHEST STAKES

The social ecosystem of ENM can be a wonderful source of joy. It can also be a minefield for those with invisible illnesses. When the social currency is high energy and effortless charm, it can feel like there is no room for a low-spoon day or a panic attack.

This "fun vibe" trap can be deadly. It leads people to mask their pain, push past their limits, and self-medicate. Your friend's constant substance use might not just be them "partying hard"; it could be a sign of unmanageable pain they feel they cannot share.

Let's talk about the unspeakable, because it touches our communities with heartbreaking frequency. The pressure to perform wellness can have the most tragic of consequences. Suicide is often the final act of a person who felt their pain was an unacceptable burden on others. When we lose one of our own to this silent battle, the grief is immense. Perhaps the most powerful way to honor the person we lost is to commit to learning from their tragic end so we can better protect those who are still struggling. Honoring them means learning the warning signs—the social withdrawal, the increased substance use, the quiet signs of desperation. It means creating a community where it is safe to not be okay, where asking for help is not a social faux pas, but a brave act of connection. We owe it to those we've lost, and to those who are still struggling, to do better.

BEYOND ABLEIST AUTONOMY: THE CARE WEB

In response to a world that prizes a toxic form of self-sufficiency, activists in the Disability Justice movement have developed a powerful alternative: the concept of a **"care web."**

A healthy polycule can create its own version of this. It's a network where multiple partners and community members contribute to the well-being of the partner in pain. This distributes the labor of care, preventing one person from becoming the sole caregiver. This model of interdependent care is a radical act. It directly challenges both ableist notions that we should all be able to "go it alone," and the mononormative assumption that one romantic partner should be the sole source of all support. It is the practical, life-saving application of being a real community.

ACCESS INTIMACY: THE DEEPEST FORM OF CARE

One of the most insidious aspects of ableism is the way it desexualizes disabled people. An ethical ENM practice must actively fight this by centering the autonomy and desirability of the disabled partner. This begins with practicing **access intimacy**.

Coined by disability justice advocate Mia Mingus, access intimacy is the profound connection you build when you "get" your partner's access needs so well that they don't have to constantly explain or advocate for themselves. It is the profound, soul-deep relief of not having to fight for their basic comfort and humanity in your relationship. It is the feeling of being truly seen. It's a partner who, without being asked, chooses a quiet restaurant because they know you get sensory overload, or who suggests a movie night at home because they can see you're on a low-spoon day.

This proactive care is the foundation of access intimacy. It means shifting from the ableist assumption of "If they wanted to see me, they'd make the energy," to the accessible practice of asking, "I understand your capacity fluctuates. What kind of date would feel good for your body right now?"

Case Study: Practicing Access Intimacy

Jess has a chronic pain condition that causes fluctuating fatigue. Their nesting partner, Alex, often helps with practical tasks. Their other partner, Sam, lives across town. Sam has learned to practice access intimacy. Before planning a date, Sam always texts: "Hey! Thinking of you. Checking in on spoon levels for this week. Would a date out be joyful, or would a quiet night in with takeout feel better for your body?" This communicates, "I want to be with you, and I am willing to build our time together around your needs." This is access intimacy in action.

NO-BULLSHIT TL;DR

- Many of the most profound illnesses are invisible. Your community is filled with people fighting battles you cannot see. Act accordingly.

- The pressure to "perform wellness" is a deadly trap that can contribute to suicide. The most radical act of community care is creating spaces where it is safe to not be okay.

- Learn Spoon Theory. Your partner isn't "flaky"; they are managing a finite budget of energy. Respecting their capacity is a fundamental act of love.

- Build "care webs," not just polycules. True community is about showing up for each other with interdependent care.

- Practice access intimacy. Anticipating your partners' needs is one of the most profound and loving ways to say, "I see you."

CHAPTER 32: IDENTITY, MARGINALIZATION, & POWER

YOUR RELATIONSHIPS DON'T EXIST IN A VACUUM

There's a sentiment you'll sometimes hear in ENM spaces, often from people who hold a great deal of privilege: "I don't want to make it political. I just want to love who I love."

That's an understandable sentiment. It's also a fantasy—a thought that can only be had from a position of profound privilege— the privilege of being able to ignore the very political forces that grant you the safety to love freely in the first place. If you are practicing Ethical Non-Monogamy, you are already engaging in a political act.

This isn't about performative wokeness or using social justice jargon to win arguments. It's about seeing the water you're swimming in. It's about understanding how power, privilege, and oppression shape who gets to feel safe, visible, desirable, and free in this lifestyle—and who is systematically ignored, fetishized, or excluded.

THIS ISN'T APOLITICAL; IT WAS BORN FROM POLITICS

The modern practice of ENM did not spring from the minds of tech bros in Silicon Valley. Its roots are deeply entangled with decades of radical political movements. It stands on the shoulders of:

- **LGBTQ+ Resistance,** which created models of "chosen family" as a survival strategy.

- **Black Feminist Ethics,** which critiqued the possessiveness of traditional monogamy and offered expansive visions of community care.

- **Disability Justice Activism,** which introduced concepts like "access intimacy" and interdependent care.

- **Anarchist and Anti-Capitalist Thought,** which critiques how the state turns relationships into instruments of property and control.

To practice ENM ethically requires being honest about the world we all live in.

SEEING THE STRUCTURES: HOW POWER SHOWS UP IN ENM

Privilege isn't about being a bad person; it's about recognizing the invisible advantages the system grants you. It's the social equivalent of being born right-handed in a world designed for right-handed people—you don't notice the advantages until you see someone left-handed struggling to use the scissors. It shows up in the answers to these questions: Who gets believed when they name harm? Whose anger is seen as righteous, and whose is seen as "aggressive"? Who feels safe at events, and who is made to feel like a fetish object?

ACKNOWLEDGING YOUR OWN PRIVILEGE IS NOT ABOUT FEELING GUILTY; IT IS ABOUT TAKING RESPONSIBILITY FOR THE UNEARNED ADVANTAGES YOUR IDENTITY GIVES YOU IN A SYSTEM THAT IS NOT FAIR. IT'S ABOUT USING THAT ADVANTAGE TO MAKE SPACES SAFER FOR EVERYONE

- **If you hold White Privilege:**

- What it is: The unearned social, economic, and systemic advantage of being white in a society structured by racial inequality.

- How it shows up: You can likely navigate ENM spaces without being racially fetishized (unlike many people of color), and your motives are less likely to be questioned based on stereotypes.

- Your responsibility is to: Listen without defensiveness when people of color share their experiences of racism or microaggressions. Actively interrupt racist jokes or fetishizing comments, even when it's uncomfortable. Use your voice to advocate for diversity and inclusion at events.

- **If you hold Cisgender Privilege:**

- What it is: The advantage of having a gender identity that matches the sex you were assigned at birth (e.g., you are not transgender).

- How it shows up: You never have to worry about being misgendered, whether your ID will be questioned at a club, or if a space will have gender-neutral bathrooms. Your identity is treated as the default.

- Your responsibility is to: Normalize sharing your pronouns in introductions ("Hi, I'm Alex, and my pronouns are he/him"). If someone is misgendered, gently and politely correct the person who made the mistake. Advocate for trans-inclusive policies and gender-neutral facilities at events.

- **If you hold Able-bodied Privilege:**

- What it is: The advantage of having a body and mind that function in ways our society considers "standard," free from chronic illness, disability, or neurodivergence.

- How it shows up: You can assume most venues will be physically accessible to you. You don't have to budget your "spoons" or worry that a high-energy party will leave you exhausted for days. Your capacity is seen as the norm.

- Your responsibility is to: Recognize that "capacity" is not universal. When planning events, proactively ask, "Is this venue wheelchair accessible? Does it have a quiet space for people who get overstimulated?" Believe people when they say they don't have the energy to do something, and practice the "access intimacy" we discussed in the previous chapter.

YOUR IDENTITY IS NOT A VENDING MACHINE

Your identity is a complex tapestry. You might be monogamish with your nesting partner, have a BDSM kink you explore with a play partner, and be bicurious. These are layers of who you are. But in the dating world, labels can be flattened into a set of expectations, as if your identity is a button someone can push to get what they want.

Do not let anyone weaponize your identity against you, with manipulative lines like: "You're not really bisexual if you don't find me attractive." This is a coercive tactic designed to shame you into compliance. Your sexual orientation is your own to define; it does not obligate you to be attracted to everyone who fits a certain category.

Your Labels are a Map, Not a Menu

Your identity is a complex, evolving map of your inner world. You might be monogamish with your nesting partner, bicurious, and a submissive who only plays with women. These are all true things about you. They are pointers toward the landscape of your desires.

But in the dating world, that map is often treated like a menu at a restaurant. A stranger sees a label on your profile— "bisexual," "submissive," "pansexual"—and thinks they can point to it and say, "I'll have that."

You do not owe anyone a performance of your identity. You do not owe them access to a part of you just because you have named it. Your complex inner world is something a trusted partner gets to discover over time, not something a stranger is entitled to as a checklist.

This is the danger of signals like the colored wristbands sometimes used at play parties. Let's say a green wristband means "open to being approached."

- The respectful person sees the green band and understands it as a conversation starter. It gives them permission to walk up and say, "Hi, I saw your wristband. Would you be interested in chatting?"

- The entitled person sees the green band and treats it as consent. They see it as a permission slip to walk up and put their hands on you, assuming that your signal was a blanket invitation for their specific actions.

This is the ultimate bullshit.

To see a signal and assume it gives you permission to act is to erase the other person's humanity. Your identity is your truth; it is not their key to your body. Consent not a label. Consent is always specific: negotiated with a person, about an act, in a moment.

This can sound like:

- "You're not really pansexual if you're not attracted to me." (This is a coercive tactic that weaponizes your identity against you.)

- "Your profile says you're a submissive. You should be kneeling for me." (This is a demand for a performance, not a request for connection.)

Your labels are there to help you find people who might be traveling in the same direction. They are a map to your potential, not a menu of services you are obligated to provide.

YOUR JOB: NAVIGATING PRIVILEGE WITHOUT WEAPONIZING GUILT

If you're reading this and feeling defensive or ashamed, pause. That's a normal reaction. It is the discomfort of seeing an old, unexamined script for the first time. You are not a bad person for having privilege. You are, however, responsible for what you do with it. Guilt is a useless emotion because it focuses on your feelings instead of the impact on others. Accountability is what changes the room.

Accountability for the Privileged Looks Like:

- **Listen and Believe.** Your first job is to listen more than you speak. Your second job is to believe people from marginalized groups when they share their experiences of harm.

- **Interrupt Harm.** Use your voice and position to interrupt microaggressions, problematic jokes, or exclusionary behavior. Your silence is complicity.

- **Accept Correction Gracefully.** When you are corrected, your only job is to say, "Thank you for telling me. I will do better." Do not get defensive.

- **Do Your Own Homework.** Do not expect marginalized people to be your educators. Your education is your own responsibility.

NO-BULLSHIT TL;DR

- Your relationships do not exist in a vacuum. Acknowledging the reality of power and privilege is a non-negotiable part of ethical practice.

- Your identity is your truth, not a vending machine for someone else's desires. A label is a map, not a menu.

- Your identity also does not obligate you to be attracted to anyone. Consent is always specific, personal, and negotiated in the moment.

- If you hold privilege, your job is not to feel guilty, but to be accountable. This means listening more than you speak, accepting correction with grace, and actively working to make spaces safer for everyone.

CHAPTER 33: COMMUNITY, BELONGING, & OTHER BULLSHIT

FINDING YOUR PEOPLE, SURVIVING THE POLITICS, & KNOWING WHEN TO BOUNCE

No one thrives in ENM alone. You can read all the books and have the most self-aware polycule on the planet, and still feel like you're yelling into the void. The world outside is not built for our relationships. This is why we seek community—for the profound relief of walking into a room and not having to explain the basic geometry of our lives.

But here's the no-bullshit truth: ENM communities are not magical, enlightened utopias. They are just collections of humans. And wherever humans gather, we bring our full, messy selves with us: our cliques, our gossip, our power plays, and our unhealed trauma.

This is your guide to finding your people, navigating the inevitable messes with integrity, knowing when the healthiest community is the one you build yourself, and the courage to walk away from one.

WHY COMMUNITY MATTERS: IT'S SURVIVAL INFRASTRUCTURE

In monogamy, social support is often built in. In ENM, you often start with a deficit. Community isn't just a social extra; it's survival infrastructure. A good community provides validation, a shared language, mentors, and a safe harbor to celebrate joys and grieve losses.

But this desperate search for belonging can make us vulnerable. When you've been starved for acceptance, a place that finally welcomes you can feel like an oasis. This deep, human need to fit in can cause us to overlook red flags and tolerate behavior we would never accept elsewhere.

THE SHADOW CURRENCY: GOSSIP, OSTRACISM, & WEAPONIZED "CONCERN"

Gossip is the shadow currency of every community, but in ENM, it often comes disguised as ethical concern or processing.

Do not be the person who sabotages someone's reputation out of jealousy. Do not be the person who weaponizes a minor misstep to publicly call someone out when your real motivation is jealousy. This is not ethical accountability; it is cowardly, passive-aggressive revenge.

And let's be clear about the performance of perfect enlightenment. Do not be the person who goes around saying, "I never get jealous." This is almost always a lie. It's social posturing that creates an environment where people who are having a genuinely hard time feel ashamed to admit it. It turns a community into a stage for performative enlightenment, not a safe harbor for real, messy humans. Being honest about your struggles is what creates real community.

While whisper networks can be a vector for gossip, for many women and marginalized people, they are also a critical, life-saving survival tool in communities that lack formal accountability. The goal is not to eliminate backchannels but to use them with integrity.

NAVIGATING THE SOCIAL FABRIC: THE SMALL POND

As you spend more time in a local ENM community, you will quickly realize it's not a vast ocean; it's a small, interconnected pond. The person you're interested in today was dating your friend six months ago. This requires you to move with long-term integrity. Your reputation follows you. Respect the aftermath of breakups and give people space to heal.

IDENTIFYING UNSAFE SPACES: THE MISSING STAIR

Unfortunately, some ENM scenes operate less like supportive communities and more like a high school cafeteria. The most dangerous figure in a toxic scene is the **"missing stair"**—a term famously coined by the blogger Cliff Pervocracy. It describes an influential person whom everyone in the group knows is harmful, but whom they all silently agree to "step over" to avoid drama. The presence of a missing stair, often propped up by enablers who benefit from their proximity to power, is the ultimate sign of a community that prioritizes the comfort of the powerful over the safety of the vulnerable.

If you find yourself in a space with a missing stair, unaccountable leaders, or a clique of the performatively "polycool," understand this: it is not your job to fix them.

Do not waste your energy trying to reform a system designed to protect its most harmful members. The most radical act of self-love and community care you can perform is not to fight a battle you cannot win, but to turn around, walk away, and refuse to let them consume your light. **Your safety is more important than their scene.**

NO-BULLSHIT TL;DR

- Community is often survival infrastructure, not a social luxury. Your need to belong is real and valid, but it can also make you vulnerable.

- Beware of gossip disguised as "ethical concern" and enlightenment used as a performance. Real community is built on the courage to be messy and imperfect together.

- Popularity is not the same as integrity. Watch for the "missing stair"–the harmful person everyone protects. The presence of enablers is the ultimate sign of an unsafe space.

- Your safety is more important than fitting in. If you can't find the community you need, and the courage to walk away from one.

CHAPTER 34: COMMON ETHICAL TRAPS

AND HOW TO CLIMB OUT WITH YOUR INTEGRITY INTACT

No one shows up to Ethical Non-Monogamy hoping to hurt someone, neglect a partner, or turn their love life into a dumpster fire of anxiety and resentment. We all start with the best of intentions.

But the truth is, you can read five books and set ten perfectly worded agreements, and you will still, at some point, find yourself caught. You will stumble into a predictable trap that countless others have stumbled into before. These are not signs of personal failure; they are the well-worn grooves of our collective inherited scripts. They are the traps our culture lays for us, baited with our deepest fears, our unexamined insecurities, and the intoxicating allure of novelty. These traps rarely exist in isolation; they are often interconnected. A partner blinded by the NRE Wrecking Ball, for instance, often becomes a Squeaky Hinge.

This is a field guide to those common patterns. If you recognize yourself in one of them, take a breath. This does not mean your relationship is doomed or that you are a bad person. It means you are normal. The goal is not to shame you for the patterns you've already fallen into, but to help you see the mechanics behind them so you can climb out with more grace and co-create a healthier dynamic moving forward.

A FIELD GUIDE TO COMMON ENM TRAPS

The NRE Wrecking Ball

- **It feels like:** "This new connection is so effortless and perfect, unlike my old, complicated relationship. This must be my real soulmate!"

- **The No-Bullshit Reality:** This is the intoxicating, reality-distorting high of New Relationship Energy. It causes a person to lose sight of self-regulation, prioritizing novelty over integrity and neglecting established connections. It is a classic failure to manage your finite resources.

The Unicorn Hunt

- **It feels like:** "We just need to find that one special person who will fit perfectly into our lives and not have any inconvenient needs of their own."

- **The No-Bullshit Reality:** This is the trap of treating a single person as an accessory to fulfill a couple's fantasy, not as a whole person. It is an act of objectification rooted in toxic couple privilege.

The Gilded Cage of Rules

- **It feels like:** "If I can just make enough rules, I won't have to feel anxious anymore."

- **The No-Bullshit Reality:** This is the trap of using restrictions not as genuine safety measures, but as a way to manage your own anxiety by controlling a partner. It stifles trust, violates autonomy, and is a hallmark of unethical, prescriptive hierarchy.

The Squeaky Hinge

- **It feels like:** "Why can't my two partners just get along? It's so stressful being in the middle."

- **The No-Bullshit Reality:** This is a common failure mode where a hinge partner, often due to conflict avoidance, creates friction between their partners through poor communication or triangulation. The way out is not to manage them, but to take radical ownership of your own conduct.

The Emotional Hot Potato

- **It feels like:** "Your feelings are your problem, not mine. You need to do your own work."

- **The No-Bullshit Reality:** This is where the concept of personal responsibility is twisted into a weapon of relational neglect. A partner shoves the other's pain back at them, refusing to engage with the impact of their own actions.

The Relationship Spackle

- **It feels like:** "Our relationship is struggling. Maybe opening it up will bring some excitement back."

- **The No-Bullshit Reality:** This is the trap of using a new person or the thrill of opening up as a patch for pre-existing problems. It is like trying to fix a cracked foundation by applying a new coat of paint. It will always fail.

The "Might as Well" Gambit

- **It feels like:** A small boundary was crossed—maybe an unplanned, drunken kiss at a party. Instead of stopping and taking accountability, the person who crossed the line decides to double down.

- **It sounds like:** "Well, the damage is already done, so we might as well go all the way."

- **The No-Bullshit Reality:** This is not a clumsy exploration; it is a cowardly abdication of responsibility. It uses a minor misstep as a premeditated excuse to justify a much larger betrayal.

THE "MUTUALLY ASSURED DESTRUCTION" PLOY

- **It feels like:** Your partner has cheated, and now they are pressuring you to do the same thing to neutralize their own guilt.

- **It sounds like:** "If I can get them to do it too, then they can't be mad at me."

- **The No-Bullshit Reality:** This is a manipulative tactic designed to create shared guilt. It's an attempt to evade accountability by making you complicit in the betrayal.

The Transactional Tollbooth

- **It feels like:** Your partner wants to open the relationship, but you are hesitant, so they turn your consent into a transaction.

- **It sounds like:** "If you want me to agree to you seeing other people, you have to do this with me first."

- **The No-Bullshit Reality:** This isn't a negotiation; it's a hostage situation. Consent given under this kind of pressure is not consent; it is compliance.

The Premeditated Permission Slip

- **It feels like:** Your partner is being incredibly generous by proactively offering you a "free pass."

- **It sounds like:** "You're going on that business trip? You should have some fun! I totally support you."

- **The No-Bullshit Reality:** The manipulation is revealed when they come back and say, "Now, it's my turn." This was never about your pleasure; it was a premeditated strategy to get what they wanted without having to navigate your genuine feelings.

  A Critical Note on Coercion: It is entirely possible to be manipulated into one of these situations and then discover that you actually thrive in non-monogamy. Your positive outcome, however, does not erase the deep ethical failure of how the relationship was opened. You are allowed to enjoy the destination while still acknowledging that the way you were forced onto the path was wrong.

CLIMBING OUT OF THE TRAPS: A GUIDE TO REPAIR

Recognizing yourself in one of these patterns can bring up a hot wave of shame. Breathe. That feeling is a sign that you care. It's the fuel for change, not a verdict of failure. The goal isn't perfection; it's repair.

A Four-Step Guide to Repair

1. **Name the Pattern (Acknowledge).** You cannot change what you do not name. The first step is to acknowledge the pattern, out loud, to the people it has affected. Use the language from this chapter: "I've realized I've been acting like a 'Squeaky Hinge.' "

2. **Own the Impact (Apologize).** Using the tools from Chapter 13, offer a real apology. This is not about your intentions; it is about their experience. "I know that my poor communication has created resentment between you two, and I am so sorry for the stress I've caused."

3. **Co-Create a New Strategy (Collaborate).** Repair is a collaborative act. You cannot fix this alone. Ask for help: "What would better support look like from me? How can we co-design a communication plan that works for everyone?"

4. **Demonstrate Change Through Action (Integrate).**
   An apology is just the ticket to the dance. The real
   work is in showing up differently, consistently, over
   time. This is how trust is rebuilt.

NO-BULLSHIT TL;DR

- Everyone messes up. Common ethical traps—like NRE-driven
  chaos, unicorn hunting, or using polyamory as a "fix"—are
  predictable patterns, not personal failings.

- These traps are usually born from the unexamined, inherited
  scripts of the Monogamy Mindset: fear, scarcity, and a lack of
  self-regulation.

- The antidote is a commitment to radical self-awareness, clear
  communication, and uncompromising accountability.

- Recognizing you've fallen into a trap doesn't make your
  relationship a failure. It makes you a normal person with the
  knowledge and the opportunity to repair.

CHAPTER 35: COERCIVE CONTROL

WHEN FREEDOM'S LANGUAGE BECOMES A CAGE

Let's talk about the most dangerous person you will ever meet in this world.

They will not look like a monster. They will look like your soulmate. They will be charismatic, insightful, and will seem to understand your deepest wounds. They will speak the language of therapy, of consent, of conscious communication, better than you do. And they will use that beautiful, compassionate language to dismantle your reality, piece by piece.

This is the face of coercive control.

This chapter is not about a bad date or a clumsy partner. It is about a specific and insidious form of abuse that is particularly dangerous in ENM and "conscious" communities. It is not about a single act of violence; it is about a systematic process of domination. It's about how an abuser takes the very tools of liberation this book teaches—vulnerability, accountability, boundaries—and twists them into a cage designed for your compliance.

Your safety is more important than anyone's vocabulary. This chapter is a guide to spotting the difference between real freedom and a cage that has been painted to look like it.

Abuse is not just mind games. Any partner who lays a hand on you in anger, throws things, punches walls, or uses their physical size to intimidate you is an abuser. Scaring someone into doing something— whether canceling a date or performing a sex act—through a menacing presence or a veiled threat is coercive control. It is abuse. Period.

THE SLOW BOIL: HOW COERCIVE CONTROL WORKS

Abuse rarely starts with a fist. It starts with a flower. It's a process of escalating control, and it's designed to be confusing. If you're asking yourself, "Am I crazy, or is this abuse?" you are likely in the middle of it. Understanding its phases is your best defense.

Phase 1: The Seduction (Love Bombing & Weaponized Vulnerability)

The cycle begins with **Love Bombing**: an overwhelming, premature flood of affection designed to create a fast, intense attachment. It sounds like, "I've never met anyone like you. Let's start a polycule this week."

This is often paired with **Weaponized Vulnerability**. The person shares their deepest traumas with you very early on, creating a false sense of intimacy. It's a tactic. It makes you feel special and makes it harder to question them later, because you feel you owe them compassion. This cycle of intense affection followed by manipulation is what forges a **trauma bond**—a powerful, addictive attachment that makes it incredibly difficult to leave a relationship you know is harmful.

Phase 2: The Isolation (Weaponized Boundaries & "Woke Talk")

Once the bond is forged, the isolation begins, often disguised in the language of safety.

- **Weaponized Boundaries:** An abuser uses the language of boundaries to control your life. A healthy boundary is about their own actions ("If you yell, I will leave"). A weaponized boundary is a rule about yours ("My boundary is that you can't be friends with your ex").

- **Weaponized "Woke Talk":** They use social justice or therapeutic jargon to make your support system feel toxic. Friends who question the relationship are labeled "mononormative." This isn't protection; it's a tactic to cut you off from anyone who might give you a reality check.

Phase 3: The Erosion (Gaslighting and Weaponized Language)

With your support system weakened, the abuser begins to erode your sense of reality.

- **Gaslighting & The FOG:** Gaslighting is manipulating someone into doubting their own sanity. It thrives in what therapist Susan Forward famously named **the FOG: Fear,**

Obligation, and Guilt. The abuser creates a constant state of low-level anxiety where you feel **afraid** to upset them, **obligated** to meet their needs, and **guilty** for having your own.

- **The "Tool vs. Weapon" Dynamic:** This is where the language of our community is turned against you. Your legitimate feelings are dismissed with phrases like, "That's your trauma response speaking," or "You're just projecting." These are not invitations to grow; they are tactics to make you believe the problem is never their behavior, but always your reaction.

Table 35.1: The Tool vs. The Weapon–A Litmus Test for Manipulative Language

The Concept	As an Ethical Tool (It Builds Connection)	As a Weapon (It Breaks Trust)
Consent	Empowerment: "I want to ensure we both feel a whole-hearted 'yes'."	Evasion: "I don't consent to this conversation." (Used as a shield to avoid accountability).
Vulnerability	Connection: "I'm sharing this so you can understand me better."	Deflection: "I only did that because of my trauma." (Used as an excuse for harmful behavior).
Boundaries	Self-Protection: "If you continue to yell, I will leave the room."	Control: "My boundary is that you can't be friends with your ex." (A rule disguised as a boundary).
The Core Intent	To Deepen Connection & Mutual Understanding	To Win, Control, or Evade Accountability

Phase 4: Overt Control

The first three phases are the psychological groundwork. Once your reality is warped and your support system is gone, the control can become more overt, including financial control or physical intimidation.

Case Study: Coercive Control In Action

Jen told her partner, Mark, that she was going on a date. Mark didn't yell; he just stood up and blocked the doorway. He crossed his arms. *"You really think that's a good idea?"*, his voice quiet. He didn't have to touch her, but she felt trapped. Her body went into high alert. Her desire to go on the date evaporated, replaced by a desperate need to make the confrontation end. *"You're right,"* she said. *"It's a bad idea. I'll cancel."*

He didn't have to hit her. He just had to make her afraid. That is control. That is abuse.

TRUST YOUR GUT: A SOMATIC RED FLAG CHECKLIST

Sometimes, your conscious mind can be tied in knots by sophisticated gaslighting. But your body knows the truth. Your nervous system cannot be gaslit. It doesn't understand "radical honesty"; it understands safety and threat. If you consistently feel anxious, confused, foggy, or exhausted around a person, your body is telling you that you are not safe.

GETTING OUT: A PROTOCOL FOR RECLAIMING YOUR SANITY

If you recognize these patterns, your goal is not to fix the other person. Your goal is to get out safely.

1. **Stop Explaining Yourself.** You do not need their permission to leave. "No" is a complete sentence. So is "I'm leaving."

2. **Document.** Save screenshots of manipulative texts. Write down specific examples of what happened. This is for you, so you can read it later when you start to doubt your own memory.

3. **Reach Out to a "Before" Friend.** Connect with a trusted friend from outside the toxic dynamic. Let them be your anchor to reality.

4. **Go "Gray Rock."** Communicate only when absolutely necessary (e.g., for co-parenting). Keep responses brief, informative, and devoid of emotion.

5. **Block, Mute, and Create Distance.** You need a clean break to hear your own voice again.

6. **Seek Professional Support.** Find a therapist trained in narcissistic abuse or relational trauma.

7. **Make a Safety Plan.** If you fear for your physical safety in any way, do not do this alone. Contact a domestic violence hotline or a trusted friend to help you create a plan for leaving safely.

NO-BULLSHIT TL;DR

- Abuse is about power and control, not relationship structures. Polyamory is not a shield against abuse.

- Abuse is a process. It often starts with love bombing and escalates to isolation and control, using the beautiful language of therapy and ENM as a weapon.

- Your body knows. Your nervous system cannot be gaslit. If you consistently feel anxious, confused, or afraid around a person, you are not safe.

CHAPTER 36: CULTS, CHARISMA, & CONTROL

WHEN THE COMMUNITY BECOMES A RELIGION

You didn't come to Ethical Non-Monogamy to be controlled. You didn't seek out alternative ways of loving to be exploited or manipulated. You came seeking freedom.

And yet, with a terrifying regularity, people on this path find themselves entangled in groups that feel less like a liberating community and more like a high-control group.

This isn't about headline-grabbing cults with compounds and matching sneakers. It's about the subtle ways charismatic control can show up in everyday relationships, polycules, and communities— especially ones that use the language of "empowerment" and "consciousness." This is the modern face of the charismatic abuse we discussed in the history chapter—the same patterns of control, just wrapped in a new, enlightened vocabulary. It's about the self-proclaimed poly guru, the tantra school with no ethical oversight, or the tightly knit poly family that slowly isolates you from the outside world.

THE SEEKER'S VULNERABILITY

Our communities can be fertile ground for these dynamics. People often come to ENM because they are "seekers"–looking for a better way to live and love after being failed by the mainstream scripts we've been deconstructing throughout this book. Your hope for a better way is not a weakness; it is a sign of your courage. But that inherent hope can make you uniquely vulnerable to a charismatic figure who claims to have all the answers. These groups don't prey on the weak; they prey on the hopeful.

WHAT ACTUALLY IS A "CULT"? IT'S ABOUT CONTROL, NOT BELIEFS

A cult isn't defined by its beliefs. A group becomes a cult–or exhibits cultic dynamics–based on its **structure of control**. Experts like Steven Hassan, who created the BITE model (Behavior, Information, Thought, and Emotional control), identify four overlapping areas of control:

1. **Behavior Control:** The group dictates how you live, from your diet to who you can date, often under the guise of "energetic alignment."

2. **Information Control:** Outside information is forbidden. Contact with friends or family who are "not evolved" is discouraged. Critical books are labeled "low-vibrational."

3. **Thought Control:** Doubt is reframed as a personal failing. When you raise a valid concern, you are told, "That's just your ego resisting growth," or "You're stuck in a scarcity mindset."

4. **Emotional Control:** Praise (love bombing) and shame are manipulated. This looks like intense love bombing when you first join, followed by public shaming or shunning for those who question the leader.

A FIELD GUIDE TO RED FLAGS IN "CONSCIOUS" COMMUNITIES

If you see a cluster of these, your alarm bells should be screaming.

- **The Charismatic, Unaccountable Leader:** A central figure who seems to have all the answers but has no peers, only followers. Any challenge to their authority is met with gaslighting.

- **Love Bombing and Instant Intimacy:** You are showered with praise when you first join. This isn't genuine connection; it's a grooming tactic.

- **An "Us vs. Them" Mentality:** The group sees itself as more evolved than the outside world, justifying isolating members from friends and family who "just don't get it."

- **The Weaponization of "Enlightened" Language:** Your boundary becomes a "trauma wall," and your discomfort is just "your ego resisting growth."

- **No Real Path for Conflict Resolution:** When actual harm occurs, there is no fair process. The outcome always protects the person with more power.

- **Financial or Labor Exploitation:** "Commitment" to the group starts to involve expensive workshops or free labor for the leader's business. This is where the "gift vs. transaction" line we discussed in Chapter 25 is deliberately blurred.

GETTING OUT: A PRACTICAL GUIDE TO RECLAIMING YOUR MIND

If you recognize these patterns, your goal is not to fix the group. Your goal is to **get out safely.**

1. **Give Yourself Permission to Have Been Wrong.** The first step is allowing yourself to think, "What if I was wrong about this?" This is not an admission of failure; it is an act of profound courage and self-liberation.

2. **Reconnect with a Trusted Outsider.** Identify one trusted friend or family member from your "before" life. Let them be your anchor to reality.

3. **Educate Yourself in Private.** On a safe device, read about coercive control. Learning the terminology of thought reform gives you a framework to understand what is happening.

4. **Do Not Confront the Group or Leader.** Do not announce you are leaving. This is a critical safety rule. They will use love bombing, guilt, and shame to pull you back in.

5. **Create a Phased Exit Plan.** Quietly reduce your involvement. Become "busy" and unavailable for events. Blame external factors ("work is really demanding").

6. **Seek Specialized Professional Support.** When you are safely able to, find a therapist trained in cult recovery or relational trauma.

7. **Practice Self-Forgiveness.** Leaving a high-control group can come with a tidal wave of shame or embarrassment. Be kind to yourself. You were not stupid; you were hopeful. The work now is to reclaim your story and your life.

You do not need "proof" of abuse to justify leaving. You do not need to win an argument. You do not need the group's permission to exit. Your discomfort and the quiet, persistent feeling that something isn't right are valid and sufficient reasons. You are the ultimate authority on your own life. You have the right to choose your own well-being over anyone else's "truth."

NO-BULLSHIT TL;DR

- Cultic dynamics are not just about weird beliefs; they are about structures of control. They can and do show up in ENM communities, often disguised in the language of empowerment.

- Beware of any group with a charismatic, unaccountable leader who places themselves beyond critique. Charisma without accountability is a dangerous red flag.

- Your hope for a better way of living is your strength, but it can also be your vulnerability. Vet your communities as ruthlessly as you vet your partners.

- If you feel like you're disappearing, something is deeply wrong. You do not need proof to leave. Your discomfort is enough. Your autonomy is not up for negotiation.

PART 6: THE LIFECYCLE OF LOVE

CHAPTER 37: THE "GOOD ENOUGH" POLYCULE

ON REPAIR, RESILIENCE, & RADICAL ACCEPTANCE

Let's start with the most freeing truth in this entire guide, especially if you've been reading all these chapters and thinking, "I'm not good enough for this." **You will never find a perfect partner, and you will never be one.**

The people you love will be clumsy, flawed, and have a fascinating array of unhealed childhood wounds. They will have attachment styles that clash with yours. They will be bad at communicating when they're tired, and they will occasionally be selfish. So will you.

If the only people "qualified" for ENM were perfectly secure, self-actualized, trauma-free communicators, the entire community would consist of about seven people. And they'd probably be lying. The entry requirement for ethical non-monogamy is not perfection; it is a commitment to repair. The goal is a "good enough" partnership with "good enough" people who are committed to the messy, beautiful work of repair.

THE FLAWED VS. THE ABUSIVE: A CRUCIAL DISTINCTION

Your partner forgetting to text from their date is a flaw. Your partner "forgetting" to tell you they are fluid-bonded with someone else is a deception. The most important skill you can develop is the ability to distinguish between a flawed partner and an abusive one. A flawed partnership can be repaired. An abusive one must be escaped.

Giving grace to a flawed human is compassionate; making excuses for an abuser is dangerous. The difference lies in the pattern and the response to feedback. A flaw is an unexamined, inherited script acted out unconsciously. When it's brought to light, it's met with genuine remorse and a commitment to change. Abuse is a conscious or unconscious refusal to change the script, even when confronted with its harmful impact. It is a pattern of violations met with excuses, blame-shifting, and defensiveness.

Here is the difference in practice:

- A flawed partner expresses jealousy to find reassurance. An abusive partner uses jealousy to control you.

- A flawed partner makes a mistake and takes ownership. An abusive partner makes a mistake and finds a way to blame you for it.

THE ANATOMY OF A REAL REPAIR

A "good enough" relationship isn't one without problems; it's one that has a reliable process for repair.

1. **Clean Accountability:** This starts with a real apology, as we detailed in Chapter 13. The person who caused harm takes full, unambiguous ownership of their actions and the impact they had. A bullshit apology "I'm sorry you feel that way"—is not accountability; it is a manipulation.

2. **Understanding the "Why":** The person who caused harm takes on the responsibility of understanding why they made that choice. This is their work to do, often with a therapist, to identify the root of the behavior so they don't repeat it.

3. **Changed Behavior Over Time:** This is the only part that actually matters in the long run. Trust is not rebuilt with words. It is rebuilt with a consistent, demonstrated pattern of new, more trustworthy behavior.

GREEN FLAGS: THE SIGNS OF A HEALTHY FOUNDATION

A red flag is a warning sign. A **green flag** is a sign of safety, integrity, and a healthy foundation. Green flags are not indicators of a "perfect" person or relationship. They are indicators of a "good enough" one— a person or a system with a built-in capacity for honest, good-faith repair.

Green Flags in a Partner

- They speak about their exes with respect, even if the breakup was painful.

- They proactively protect time for your relationship, especially when in the throes of NRE.

- They take full accountability for their mistakes without defensiveness.

- They celebrate your other connections and express genuine compersion for your joy.

- They welcome conversations about boundaries and agreements as an act of connection.

Green Flags in a Hinge

- They are an impeccable emotional firewall, never venting to one partner about the other.

- They facilitate connection based on consent, asking what level of interaction their partners desire.

- They refuse to be a "go-between," empowering partners to build their own connections.

Green Flags in Yourself

- You can sit with your own discomfort (like jealousy) and investigate it before you externalize it.

- You can celebrate your partner's joy with another person, even if it brings up a pang of envy.

- You are able to set and hold a boundary with kindness and without apology.

- You can honestly assess your own capacity and say "no" when you are polysaturated.

A relationship landscape filled with these green flags is not one without problems. It is one where you have a deep, abiding trust that you and the people you love have the skills and the integrity to navigate those problems together.

NO-BULLSHIT TL;DR

- The goal is not a perfect relationship; it's a "good enough" one with people who are committed to the messy, beautiful work of repair.

- Learn to distinguish between a flawed partner (who makes mistakes and is willing to learn) and an abusive partner (who repeats harmful patterns and refuses to change).

- Real repair requires three things: clean accountability, a deep understanding of the "why" behind the mistake, and a consistent pattern of changed behavior over time.

- Look for green flags. They are not signs of perfection, but of a healthy capacity for repair. This is the true foundation of a resilient and lasting love.

CHAPTER 38: DE-ESCALATION

THE ART OF THE GRACEFUL DOWNSHIFT

The Monogamy Mindset gives us an all-or-nothing script for relationships: you are either escalating toward marriage, or you are "broken up." There is no room for a middle ground. Non-monogamy, and the unbundling of different types of connection, offers a more nuanced spectrum of possibilities. Not all endings are amputations. Sometimes, a relationship doesn't need to end; it just needs to change shape.

De-escalation is the conscious, intentional process of shifting a relationship from a form of higher intensity to one of lower intensity, not to end it, but to save it by finding a more authentic and sustainable shape.

WHY DE-ESCALATE?

People choose to de-escalate for many valid reasons. It is not a breakup in slow motion; it's a proactive choice to find a more sustainable form for a connection you still value.

- **A Shift in Life Priorities:** A demanding new career or the needs of aging parents can change your capacity.

- **A Change in Compatibility:** You may realize you aren't compatible as nesting partners but would be wonderful as deeply connected friends.

- **To Reduce Relational Stress:** Sometimes, the current level of entanglement is simply causing more stress than joy.

THE DE-ESCALATION PROTOCOL

This process requires the same level of care as a breakup, if not more.

1. **State Your Need Clearly and Kindly.** Frame it from your perspective: "I love you and value our connection. I've realized that my capacity has changed, and the level of intensity we have right now isn't sustainable for me. I would like to talk about shifting our relationship from lovers to deeply connected friends."

2. **Grieve the Old Form.** Allow yourself and your partner to grieve the loss of the relationship you had. It is a real loss, even if you are not losing the person entirely.

3. **Explicitly Redefine the New Form.** Have a clear, detailed conversation about what the new relationship will look like. How often will you see each other? What will communication look like?

4. **Give It Time and Space.** The transition period will be awkward. You may need a period of low or no contact to allow old patterns to fade before you can successfully build the new one.

ACKNOWLEDGING THE PAIN OF BEING DE-ESCALATED ON

Let's be clear: being told someone wants to de-escalate can feel exactly like a breakup. Your partner's intention may be to preserve the connection, but the impact on you is still the loss of the relationship you thought you had. That is a real loss, and you are allowed to grieve it fully. Your feelings of hurt, rejection, or sadness are valid.

What happens if they say no? What if your partner says, "No, I don't want to be friends. It's this or nothing"? That is their boundary, and it must be respected. The ethical path is to honor their "no" and transition to a full breakup, even if that wasn't your initial intention. You don't get to force someone into a friendship they don't want.

Choosing to de-escalate is not a failure. It is an act of profound relational maturity. It is a courageous rejection of the "all-or-nothing" script in favor of a commitment to finding the right and true shape for a connection, rather than clinging to a form that no longer fits.

We were both in pain, but still cared for each other. We didn't want to break up, just… breathe. We moved into separate rooms. We each got a few nights a week to ourselves. We started sleeping apart, eating together, and being intentional about what we could still do well together: cohabitate, collaborate, and co-parent. This is what we told our friends. And we meant it. We still loved each other. We still do. We just didn't want the same shape of love anymore.

NO-BULLSHIT TL;DR

- De-escalation is the courageous choice to change a relationship's shape to preserve it, rather than ending it. It's a downshift, not a breakup.

- It is a rejection of the monogamous "all-or-nothing" script. Not all endings have to be amputations.

- If you are the one being de-escalated on, your grief is valid. The impact on you is a real loss, regardless of your partner's intent.

- If your partner rejects the de-escalation and chooses a full breakup, their boundary must be respected. You cannot force a friendship.

CHAPTER 39: THE AFTERMATH

NAVIGATING POLYCULE BREAKUPS, GRIEF, & RECONFIGURATION

There is no such thing as a clean breakup.

In monogamy, an ending can feel like a devastating tear in the fabric of your life. In polyamory, that tear can unravel an entire ecosystem. When one relationship ends, the shockwaves travel through a living web of metamours, shared friends, and chosen family.

The "clean break" is a myth. Navigating this is one of the hardest experiences in ENM. It requires a level of grace, compassion, and impeccable boundaries that will test even the most experienced practitioner.

THE SHATTERED WEB: THE UNIQUE PAIN OF A POLYCULE BREAKUP

A polycule breakup isn't just the loss of a romantic partner. It is often a trauma to the entire chosen family. It's a cascade of secondary losses that are often invisible to the outside world:

- **The Loss of a Metamour:** You may have developed a close, platonic friendship with your metamour, a bond that is now threatened.

- **The Loss of Community:** Shared friends may feel forced to "choose sides," and you may no longer feel welcome in the same social spaces.

- **The Stress on the Hinge:** The hinge partner is often caught in the middle, trying to support a grieving partner while maintaining their other relationships.

- **The Disruption of a "Chosen Family":** If you were in a KTP-style polycule, a breakup can feel like a divorce that shatters the entire family unit.

THE BULLSHIT OF PERFORMING HAPPINESS

Layered on top of this pain is a toxic, unspoken pressure to act like you're okay. There is a performance of enlightened happiness in some ENM communities that can be incredibly isolating. This is one of the most toxic forms of dogma in the non-monogamy world—the unspoken rule that if you were "doing it right," you wouldn't be in so much pain. This is a lie. A broken heart is a broken heart. The end of a long-term partnership is a death, and you are allowed to mourn it fully, without apology. Real strength is not in pretending you don't feel pain; it's in having the courage to feel it honestly.

The final act of a "good enough" relationship is to end it with as much integrity as possible. This requires each person to manage their role with care, with the goal of doing the least possible harm.

BREAKUP ETIQUETTE: A GUIDE TO DOING LESS HARM

This requires each person to manage their role with care.

For the person ending it: Be direct, honest, and kind. Do not soften the blow with ambiguity. Own your decision without blaming and refuse the cowardice of ghosting.

For the person being left: Honor your feelings and seek support from your own network, not from the person leaving you. It is okay to be hurt, angry, and sad.

For the hinge partner: Your responsibility is to act as an unbreachable emotional firewall. Support each of your partners individually, but do not relay messages, take sides, or make one person's grief the other's problem.

For the metamour: Your role is to offer support to your shared partner while respecting the privacy of the two people breaking up. Do not pry for details. Do not, under any circumstances, treat the breakup as a "win" for your own relationship.

NO-BULLSHIT TL;DR

- A polycule breakup is not a single amputation; it is a complex trauma to your entire chosen family, often involving a cascade of secondary losses.

- Do not perform "enlightened happiness." Your grief is valid, no matter how many other partners you have. A broken heart is a broken heart.

- Practice good breakup etiquette. The goal is not to be perfect, but to do the least possible harm. Be direct, be honest, and refuse the cowardice of ghosting.

- If you are the hinge, your final responsibility is to be an impeccable emotional firewall. Do not triangulate. Do not make one person's grief another person's problem.

CHAPTER 40: THE LAST-CHANCE ON-RAMP

NAVIGATING ENM AS A FINAL RESORT

Let's talk about one of the most common, and most dangerous, entry points into Ethical Non-Monogamy: the Hail Mary pass. It's the conversation that starts with, "Before we get a divorce, we might as well try opening up."

A relationship is on life support. One or both partners, often acting from the only script they know, see ENM not as an authentic expression of their relational philosophy, but as a last-ditch attempt to resuscitate a dying marriage. It is the final, desperate move in a game whose rules no longer work.

Can this ever be ethical? Yes. But it requires a level of radical, uncomfortable honesty that most couples in this position are not prepared for, and it requires that this honesty be extended to every new person you bring into your chaos.

THE FIRST ETHICAL TEST: HONESTY WITH YOUR PARTNER

Trying ENM before a divorce is not, in itself, unethical. The ethical failure is pretending you are doing it for any other reason. If one partner is thinking, 'This is my last attempt before I call a lawyer,' and the other is thinking, 'Great! We're finally starting our exciting polyamorous adventure,' you are building on a foundation of deceit.

The only ethical starting point is a terrifyingly vulnerable conversation:

> *"I want to be clear about where I'm at. Our relationship is not working, and I have been considering divorce. Before we go down that path, I am willing to try opening our relationship to see if a different structure can help. I need you to know that I see this as an experiment, and I don't know what the outcome will be."*

THE SECOND ETHICAL TEST: HONESTY WITH NEW PARTNERS

This is where most "Hail Mary" attempts collapse into unethical wreckage. You have a profound, non-negotiable ethical obligation to be honest with any new person you get involved with about the instability of your situation.

Leading on a new person, letting them invest their heart, and then revealing that your participation in the lifestyle was always conditional is a profound betrayal. And demanding that a new partner, who you met under the banner of ENM, must now abandon non-monogamy to "win" you away from your old relationship is a deeply coercive and unethical bait-and-switch. You are not offering them a relationship; you are offering them a prize in a competition they never agreed to enter. You are using a human being as a crowbar to pry open your marriage, and that is a profound ethical failure.

Honesty with a new partner sounds like this, from the very first date:

> *"I want to be transparent about my situation. My nesting partner and I are exploring ENM as part of a process of figuring out if our marriage can continue. I can't offer a lot of long-term stability right now, and I wanted you to have that information upfront."*

Anything less is using another person as an unwitting pawn in your own relationship drama.

NO-BULLSHIT TL;DR

- Using ENM as a last resort to save a relationship is a high-stakes gamble with a high potential for collateral damage.

- **Ethical Test #1:** Radical Honesty with Your Partner. You must both acknowledge that this is an experiment to avoid divorce, not a lifestyle transition.

- **Ethical Test #2:** Radical Honesty with New Partners. You have a non-negotiable duty to inform any new partner about the instability of your situation from the very first conversation. Anything less is deception.

- Do not use other people's hearts as leverage or spare parts for your primary relationship's crisis.

CHAPTER 41: THE OFF-RAMP

DE-TRANSITIONING TO MONOGAMY WITHOUT SHAME

You dove into the world of Ethical Non-Monogamy with an open heart. You read the books, you learned the jargon, you navigated the complexities. You built a life that was, for a time, a testament to the possibilities of loving freely.

And then, one day, you realized something terrifying and true: *You don't want this anymore.*

This chapter is a compassionate guide to the process of "de-transitioning" from non-monogamy back to monogamy. It is a validation of your right to change and a roadmap for how to do so with integrity.

IT'S NOT A FAILURE: DE-STIGMATIZING THE CHOICE

Choosing monogamy after practicing ENM is not a failure. It is not a regression. It is not proof that you were "never really poly" to begin with. In some ENM communities, there is a toxic dogma that treats non-monogamy as a more "enlightened" path, and returning to monogamy as a betrayal of that ideal. This is bullshit. The only ethical commitment of this lifestyle is to honor your authentic self, even when that self evolves. Sometimes, the most courageous choice you can make is to acknowledge that a particular path, no matter how beautiful, is no longer yours to walk.

The Conscious Choice: Why People Return to Monogamy

People choose to return to monogamy for many valid reasons. Are you exhausted by the logistical and emotional labor? Have your life priorities shifted? Do you simply find yourself longing for the focus of a monogamous partnership? Or have you met a specific partner with whom monogamy feels joyful and expansive? Whatever your reason, the key is to make the choice consciously, not from a place of fear or pressure.

A CRITICAL WARNING: THE UNETHICAL OFF-RAMP

There is a profound difference between a person consciously choosing monogamy for themselves and a person who uses a new connection as a destructive, NRE-fueled exit from an existing relationship.

This isn't always a calculated act of cruelty. Often, it's a chaotic cascade that a person fails to navigate with integrity. Let's be brutally clear about the impact. A relationship opens up. One partner meets someone new and the intoxicating rush of NRE rewrites their entire narrative. Suddenly, the polyamorous structure they once advocated for is framed as the problem. The new connection is idealized, and they announce they were "never really polyamorous." They then discard their original partner to ride off into the monogamous sunset with the replacement.

This is not an ethical de-transition. This is a devastating betrayal. It is using the freedom of ENM as a shopping mall to find your next monogamous partner while keeping your current one on the hook for emotional and logistical support. It is an act of profound disrespect.

The Moment of Truth: Navigating an Unplanned Exit

But what if you are the one who has just met someone new and feel that terrifying, undeniable clarity that you want to take that off-ramp? The desire itself doesn't make you a bad person. What you do next is what defines your character.

A CRITICAL WARNING ON NRE & IRREVERSIBLE DECISIONS

Before you say a single word to your current partner, STOP. That certainty you feel? It is real. It is also, very likely, a temporary form of insanity fueled by New Relationship Energy.

You do not make permanent, life-altering decisions when you are in a state of emotional intoxication.

The most ethical thing you can do right now is impose a mandatory cooling-off period on yourself. Do not speak to your partner about ending things for at least 30 days. Use that time to sit with the feeling. NRE is a powerful drug. The responsible path is to wait until you are sober before you decide to burn your house down.

If, after waiting, the certainty remains, you must end your current primary relationship with honesty and accountability before you escalate your new one. You owe your partner the truth. It sounds like this:

> *"I have something incredibly difficult to tell you. My journey in non-monogamy has led me to an unexpected place.*
>
> *I have met someone, and my connection with them has made me realize that I am no longer able to be in our polyamorous structure.*
>
> *I know this is a shocking and devastating betrayal of the path we were on together. I am not trying to justify it. I am taking ownership of my actions and the immense pain this is going to cause you. To do anything else would be to lie to you, and you deserve better than that. I am ending our relationship."*

They will be hurt. They will be furious. They will see you as the villain, and from their perspective, they will not be wrong. Your only job is to state your truth, own the devastating impact, and give them the space they need to heal.

NO-BULLSHIT TL;DR

- Choosing to return to monogamy is not a failure; it is a valid choice to honor your evolving needs. Your autonomy is your ultimate ethical guide.

- Do not make permanent, life-altering decisions while high on NRE. It is a temporary form of insanity. Impose a mandatory cooling-off period on yourself.

- The "unethical off-ramp"—using ENM to audition your next monogamous partner—is a profound betrayal. Do not keep one partner on the hook while you secure the next.

- If you must exit for a new relationship, the only path of integrity is to end your current relationship with honesty and full accountability before escalating the new one.

CHAPTER 42: THE FINAL TEST

GRIEF, LOSS, & THE CHOSEN FAMILY

Content Warning: This chapter discusses death and grief. If you are in a raw state or find this topic to be a trigger, please feel free to skip this chapter for now and come back when you feel ready. Your well-being comes first.

This is the chapter no one wants to need. All the other challenges in this book–jealousy, time management, breakups– are survivable. They are tests of our capacity for repair. This one is about the ultimate "no-bullshit" reality: life is finite. People get sick. People die. And when this happens in a polycule, it tests the very foundation of your chosen family in ways that nothing else can.

THE HIERARCHY OF GRIEF

In the aftermath of any death, an unofficial and often cruel "hierarchy of grief" can emerge. The nesting partner's grief is often seen as the most "valid," while the grief of a newer partner, a long-distance partner, or a beloved metamour can be minimized or dismissed.

Let's be clear, and let this be a command: Do not let anyone, including yourself, tell you that your grief is less real because your relationship was shorter, less entangled, or not romantic. A broken heart is a broken heart. You are allowed to mourn fully, without apology or justification.

THE LEGAL INVISIBILITY

As we warned in Chapter 25, without proactive legal planning, you can be rendered invisible by a system not built for you. A metamour can be barred from a hospital room by a hostile biological family. A long-term, unmarried partner can be left with no assets and no say in funeral arrangements. The healthcare proxy, the will, the living trust– these are not abstract documents; they are the final, most powerful act of love you can offer your chosen family.

THE SACRED DUTY OF REMEMBRANCE

Finally, we must talk about what we owe to those we've lost. Many of us come to these communities because we have been rejected by our families of origin or mainstream society. This community becomes our only family.

When we lose one of our own–whether to illness, accident, or the silent pain of suicide–our role is unique. The rest of the world will mourn a sanitized, incomplete version of them. Our sacred duty is to remember the person in their entirety. We are here to remember all of them: a loving, sexy, brilliant, open person.

To forget them or explain away their pain is a second death. Honoring them means we do not look away. We tell their stories. We hold space for the complexity of their lives. We learn from their struggles. We refuse to let them be erased. This is our final, most sacred responsibility as a community: to be the keepers of the whole truth of the people we loved.

NO-BULLSHIT TL;DR

- Your grief is valid. Do not let anyone—including yourself—enforce a "hierarchy of grief." A broken heart is a broken heart.

- Legal documents are not a chore; they are the final, most powerful act of love you can offer your chosen family. Do not wait.

- We have a sacred duty to be the keepers of our own stories. Remember the full, complex, beautiful truth of those we've lost, especially when the rest of the world will only remember a sanitized version.

- To forget them or explain away their pain is a second death. Our final responsibility is to remember.

CONCLUSION: YOUR VERSION OF THIS

WHAT SUCCESS LOOKS LIKE WHEN YOU DRAW YOUR OWN MAP

In the beginning, we promised you a compass, not a map. If you've made it this far, you've done the hard and courageous work of learning to use it. You have navigated the complex territory of your own heart, armed with a new understanding of your desires, your fears, and the inherited scripts you were taught about love. You have the tools. The map you draw from here is yours and yours alone.

So now what? After all the theory, the warnings, and the no-bullshit realities, what does it mean to "get it right"?

LONGEVITY IS NOT THE GOAL. INTEGRITY IS

You do not "win" at this by collecting the most partners or by staying in a relationship the longest. The old script's primary metric of success was duration: *Did it last?*

But this is a lie. A long relationship is not the same as a healthy one. The real work of love is found in the ongoing, messy, beautiful work of repair required to build a life with whole, flawed, real people.

Here, then, is the no-bullshit definition of success: Did you love with integrity? Did you communicate with courage?

And did you leave people, and yourself, more whole than when you started? If the answer is yes, you have succeeded wildly, no matter how long it lasted.

THE WORK IS HARD. THE JOY IS THE POINT

We have spent a lot of time in these pages on the hard parts: the jealousy, the broken agreements, the difficult conversations. But that work is not the point. It is the price of admission.

The point is the joy.

The accountability is what makes the connection feel safe. The integrity is what makes the intimacy feel real. The honesty is what makes the pleasure feel clean and unburdened. This is the payoff for all the hard work. It is the joy of connection without the fear of possession.

It's the profound warmth of a life built with a platonic partner who feels like home.

It's the electric, shared thrill of a swinger party, entered into with a partner you trust completely.

It's the quiet intimacy of a Tuesday night with a nesting partner, and the giddy excitement of a first kiss with someone new.

It is the expansive, guilt-free joy of watching your partner return from a date happy and whole, knowing their joy adds to the world, and to your own.

This is a love that is chosen, again and again, in all its many forms, with eyes wide open.

A FINAL WORD FOR THE CURIOUS, THE CAUTIOUS, & THE CURRENTLY IN IT

This book was our offering to you, and to our younger selves. As you put it down and walk back into your life, we leave you with this:

If you came to this book curious, may you leave with a clearer sense of your own desires and the tools to explore them safely. May you have the courage to ask for what you truly want.

If you came to this book cautious, perhaps handed to you by a partner, may you leave feeling seen, empowered, and confident in your own boundaries. May you know in your bones that your "no" is sacred and your needs are valid.

And if you are currently in it, navigating the messy realities of this life, may you leave feeling less alone, more hopeful, and equipped with a renewed commitment to the beautiful, difficult work of loving with integrity.

This path will test you—but it will also introduce you to some of the kindest, most self-aware, emotionally generous people you will ever meet. People who have chosen to love without ownership. Who speak with honesty, not cruelty. Who hold space, hold boundaries, and hold you when it all falls apart. People who will inspire you to be better.

May you meet those people. May you be one of those people.

NO-BULLSHIT TL;DR

- Success is defined by health and integrity, not longevity.

- Embrace imperfection. "Good enough" partnerships that allow for honest repair are the real win.

- Prioritize your autonomy. You are always allowed to change your mind, to evolve, and to choose your own path.

- The work is hard, but it is the foundation for a love—in all its forms—that is more honest, resilient, and joyful than the old scripts ever allowed.

APPENDICES

ACKNOWLEDGMENTS

In a book about privacy and consent, the traditional act of naming names in an acknowledgment feels like a contradiction. The work of this book was made possible by a community, and our primary responsibility is to protect that community. We therefore offer our gratitude anonymously, trusting that the people who carried us through this process will recognize themselves in these words.

To our own partners, who lived through the writing of this book with grace: thank you for your patience, for holding space for our work, and for reminding us daily that love is a practice, not a theory.

To our chosen family and the wider ENM community: thank you for the conversations, the wisdom, the shared stories of joy and heartbreak, and for creating spaces where we could learn and unlearn. This book is a reflection of the collective knowledge you have so generously shared.

To the brave souls who read the early, ugly drafts and offered the candid feedback that sharpened this book's focus and strengthened its heart: your intellectual and emotional labor was a profound gift.

ACKNOWLEDGMENTS

And, in the spirit of this book, we must also acknowledge the difficult lessons learned from painful encounters. To those who showed us, through their actions, what a lack of ethics looks like: you provided a harsh but necessary education. The clarity in these pages was forged in the fire of those experiences.

Finally, to you, the reader. Thank you for your curiosity, your courage, and your willingness to do this hard, worthwhile work. This book was always for you.

APPENDIX A: THE NO-B.S. QUICK-REFERENCE TOOLKIT

This is your cheat sheet. These are the core moves from this book in their most stripped-down form—meant for in-the-moment use. The main chapters and References carry full background and citations. Here, you just need tools you can grab fast.

THE UNF*CKABLE CONVERSATION SCRIPT

(See Chapter 8 for full context.)

Use this four-step script to talk about hard things without blame.

1. **What I noticed** *(neutral fact—camera test)*

2. **What I felt** *(an "I feel..." sentence)*

3. **What matters here** *(the value/need underneath)*

4. **My clear ask** *(specific, doable, refusable request)*

Template: "When I **noticed** [...], I **felt** [...], because **what matters** to me is [...]. Would you be willing to **[clear ask]**?"

WHEN JEALOUSY SPIKES: A 4-LINE NOTE TO SELF

(See Chapter 9 for full context.)

Use this to steady yourself before reacting.

1. **Notice:** what actually happened (camera-test facts)

2. **Name:** the primary feeling; the story you're telling

3. **Need:** the value/need being tugged (e.g., security, closeness, reassurance, respect)

4. **Next tiny step:** one self-soothe now + one clear, collaborative ask later

THE ANATOMY OF A REAL APOLOGY

(See Chapter 13 for full context.)

A complete apology includes all six elements:

1. **Name the harm:** "I broke our safer-sex agreement."

2. **Acknowledge impact:** "That betrayed your trust and put your health at risk."

3. **Express remorse:** "I'm deeply sorry for the fear and pain I caused."

4. **Commit to change:** what I will do differently next (testing, therapy, new guardrails)

5. **Invite repair needs:** "What would help you begin to feel safer?"

6. **Accept the outcome:** repair isn't owed; the other person chooses

THE GARDEN WALKTHROUGH

(See Chapter 12 for full context.)

1. **Notice willingness.** If your partner will walk the garden with you, say so; if not, that's the first issue to address.

2. **Match scope to capacity.** Fit the length/depth to the lower-capacity partner today.

3. **Look together.** Name what's strong/beautiful, what's been ignored, and what needs a simple touch-up; don't try to fix the whole garden at once.

4. **Choose only what you both agree to.** From real bandwidth (work/family/health/money/attention), pick the few items you can actually move now.

5. **Make it actionable.** Who will do what, by when, and how you'll both know it happened; write it where you'll see it (calendar/shared note/whiteboard).

6. **Keep a light cadence.** Plan a brief glance later ("five minutes next week") to adjust.

7. **Leave facing forward.** Put one near-future plan you both want on the calendar; name any lingering feelings without trying to erase them.

CONSENT BASICS: FIVE CHECKS

(See Chapter 24 for full context.)

For consent to hold, make sure it's:

1. **Freely chosen** (no pressure, guilt, or coercion)

2. **Revocable** (anyone can change their mind at any time)

3. **Informed** (no deception or withheld info about material facts)

4. **Eager** (an active yes, not the absence of no)

5. **Specific** (yes to this thing, not blanket approval for everything else)

APPENDIX B: GLOSSARY

Language in our communities is a living, breathing thing. It evolves. Different scenes and different people will use these terms in their own unique ways. This glossary is not a final verdict on what these words "should" mean; it is a guide to how we understand and use them in this book. Think of it as a solid starting point for a conversation. When in doubt, the most ethical practice is always the simplest: ask someone what a word means to them.

A

Abuse

Any pattern of behavior—physical, sexual, emotional, financial, or psychological—used to exert power and control over another person.

No-B.S. Context: Abuse is the antithesis of consent. In ENM and kink communities, abusers may twist progressive language to mask their behavior. If you consistently feel afraid, controlled, or silenced, it's abuse, regardless of the labels used.

See Also: Coercion, Gaslighting, Love Bombing, Red Flag, Threatening Presence, Trauma Bond, Weaponized Therapy-Speak.

Access Intimacy

A disability justice concept describing the profound connection felt when someone instinctively understands and honors your access needs without being prompted.

No-B.S. Context: This goes beyond physical accommodations; it's the profound, soul-deep relief of not having to constantly explain or advocate for your basic needs. It is the feeling of being truly seen.

See Also: Spoon Theory.

Accountability

The active, ongoing, and unwavering commitment to fully owning your actions and their impact on others.

No-B.S. Context: True accountability is not a performative apology designed to quickly smooth things over. It is a demonstrable, long-term shift in behavior that rebuilds trust. It is the necessary follow-through after the words "I'm sorry."

See Also: Repair, Rupture.

Aftercare

Intentional emotional and physical support following an intense experience, such as a BDSM scene, a difficult conversation, or a swinger event.

No-B.S. Context: Aftercare is not optional; it's a non-negotiable part of ethical practice. Neglecting it is a serious red flag.

See Also: BDSM, Scene.

Agreement

A mutually crafted understanding or guideline established by partners to shape their relationship.

No-B.S. Context: An agreement is a collaborative blueprint ("what will we do?"). It is built on trust and a shared goal.

See Also: Boundary, Garden Metaphor, Rule.

Allosexual (Allo)

Describes individuals who experience sexual attraction. It is the antonym of asexual.

No-B.S. Context: This term was created to normalize asexuality by naming the alternative. Instead of "sexual" being the default and "asexual" being the deviation, "allosexual" and "asexual" are presented as two different orientations.

See Also: Asexual (Ace), Demisexual.

Amatonormativity

The widespread societal assumption that a central, exclusive, amorous relationship is a universal goal and should be privileged above all other relationship types.

No-B.S. Context: This is the force that automatically places a two-year marriage above a twenty-year friendship. It is the direct source of the Relationship Escalator script (dating → marriage → kids) and the reason single or aromantic people are often seen as "incomplete."

See Also: Monogamy Mindset, Mononormativity, Platonic Partnership, Relationship Escalator.

Anchor Partner

A partner who provides significant stability and emotional grounding, regardless of hierarchy or cohabitation status.

No-B.S. Context: This term is often preferred to "primary" by non-hierarchical individuals because it describes a feeling, not a rank.

See Also: Hierarchy, Nesting Partner, Primary Partner, Solo Polyamory.

Aromantic (Aro)

Describes individuals who experience little to no romantic attraction.

No-B.S. Context: An aromantic person is not "emotionally unavailable." They may still desire deep, non-romantic connections like QPPs.

See Also: Asexual (Ace), Queerplatonic Partnership (QPP).

Asexual (Ace)

Describes individuals who experience little to no intrinsic sexual attraction.

No-B.S. Context: Asexuality is an orientation, not a choice. Ace people can still have and enjoy sex and relationships.

See Also: Aromantic (Aro), Demisexual.

Attachment Style

Patterns of bonding and emotional response in relationships, often rooted in early experiences (e.g., secure, anxious, avoidant).

No-B.S. Context: ENM, with its multiple attachments and separations, can be a trigger minefield for insecure attachment styles. Understanding your own patterns is crucial. For a deep dive, see Jessica Fern's *Polysecure*.

See Also: Co-regulation, Jealousy.

Autonomy

The right and ability to make independent decisions about one's relationships, body, and life.

No-B.S. Context: Autonomy is the bedrock of ethical ENM. A rule or dynamic that consistently undermines a person's autonomy (like a veto) is fundamentally unethical.

See Also: Boundary, Consent, Solo Polyamory, Veto.

B

BDSM

Acronym for Bondage & Discipline, Dominance & Submission, and Sadism & Masochism. A subset of kink focused on consensual activities involving power exchange, sensation, or restraint.

See Also: D/s, Kink, Power Exchange, Scene.

BIFF Method

A communication strategy for dealing with high-conflict people, keeping responses **B**rief, **I**nformative, **F**riendly, and **F**irm.

No-B.S. Context: An essential tool for co-parenting with a hostile ex. It focuses on de-escalation by refusing to engage with accusations.

Biphobia

Prejudice or exclusion based on someone's bisexuality, especially targeting bisexual men.

No-B.S. Context: A common example is the One Penis Policy, where a straight man is fine with his female partner being with other women, but not other men.

See Also: One Penis Policy (OPP).

Boundary

A limit you set to safeguard your well-being, dictating your own actions rather than controlling others.

No-B.S. Context: A boundary is your personal fence ("If you yell, I will leave"). It is about what you will do, not what you will make them do.

See Also: Agreement, Rule.

Bull

A slang term, often used in swinging, for a man who has sex with a partnered woman, typically with the enthusiastic consent of her partner.

No-B.S. Context: This term can be ethically fraught and is often associated with racial fetishization (specifically of Black men). Its use requires awareness and a commitment to ensuring no one is being objectified.

See Also: Hotwife, Swinging.

Burnout

A state of emotional, physical, and mental exhaustion caused by prolonged stress, often from ignoring one's capacity.

No-B.S. Context: Burnout is a signal that your "output" of relational energy has exceeded your "input" for too long.

See Also: Capacity, Polysaturation.

C

Capacity

Your realistic, finite ability to invest time, energy, attention, money, and emotional labor in relationships.

No-B.S. Context: While love may feel infinite, capacity is not. Honesty about your capacity is a core ethical practice.

See Also: Burnout, Polysaturation, Spoon Theory.

Casual

A descriptor for a relationship that is intentionally kept with low levels of entanglement or long-term commitment.

No-B.S. Context: "Casual" means radically different things to different people. It is a dangerously ambiguous word in dating. Define your terms explicitly.

See Also: Agreement, Comet, Open Relationship.

Cheating

The violation of trust and foundational agreements with a partner through deception.

No-B.S. Context: Cheating is not defined by having multiple partners but by the dishonesty involved.

See Also: Agreement, Rupture.

Chosen Family

A self-selected network of people providing primary social and emotional support, beyond biological or legal ties.

No-B.S. Context: This concept originated in LGBTQ+ communities as a survival strategy.

See Also: Platonic Partnership, Queerplatonic Partnership (QPP).

Coercion

Persuading someone to act through force, threats, or relentless pressure, which undermines true consent.

No-B.S. Context: Coercion is the enemy of consent. It can be subtle, like saying, "If you loved me, you'd agree to this."

See Also: Abuse, Consent.

Commitment

A conscious, explicit, and ongoing choice to invest in the well-being and continuation of a relationship.

No-B.S. Context: In ENM, commitment is decoupled from sexual exclusivity and the Relationship Escalator, and is instead defined by the specific promises made between partners.

See Also: Agreement, Monogamy Mindset, Relationship Escalator.

Consensual Non-Monogamy (CNM)

An umbrella term, often used in academic and research contexts, for relationship models where partners agree to have multiple intimate connections.

No-B.S. Context: This book deliberately uses the term "Ethical Non-Monogamy (ENM)" instead. While consent is the non-negotiable foundation, it is the lowest possible bar. It is possible to consent to dynamics that are still unethical, dishonest, or harmful. "Ethical" implies a higher standard of care, compassion, and radical honesty, which is the core focus of this guide.

See Also: Consent, ENM (Ethical Non-Monogamy).

Co-regulation

The process through which individuals in a relationship help each other manage and soothe their emotional and physiological states.

No-B.S. Context: Co-regulation acknowledges that we are not islands; we affect each other's nervous systems. It is the opposite of the Emotional Hot Potato.

See Also: Attachment Style, Emotional Hot Potato.

Comet

A significant, emotionally intimate partner with whom contact is infrequent, often due to distance.

No-B.S. Context: The relationship is cherished for its intensity when it occurs, without the expectation of following the Relationship Escalator.

See Also: Relationship Escalator.

Compersion

Genuine, vicarious joy for a partner's happiness in their other relationships.

No-B.S. Context: Compersion is a beautiful but not mandatory feeling. It's not a sign of being "more evolved," and it can co-exist with jealousy.

See Also: Jealousy, NRE.

Consent

The ethical cornerstone of all interactions, requiring F.R.I.E.S.: **F**reely given, **R**eversible, **I**nformed, **E**nthusiastic, and **S**pecific.

No-B.S. Context: Consent is an ongoing process, not a one-time checkbox.

See Also: Abuse, Autonomy, BDSM, Coercion, Safer Sex, Safeword.

Couple-Centric

A relationship model where the primary focus is on the needs and security of a pre-existing couple, often to the detriment of other partners.

No-B.S. Context: Not inherently unethical, but this is where Couple Privilege often runs rampant.

See Also: Couple Privilege, Hierarchy, Unicorn Hunting.

Couple Privilege

Unearned social, structural, and emotional advantages held by a pre-existing couple, often used to disadvantage newer partners.

No-B.S. Context: A key dynamic to be aware of to avoid unethical hierarchy.

See Also: Couple-Centric, Hierarchy, Unicorn Hunting.

Cuckold / Cuckquean

A person who derives pleasure, often erotic, from their partner having sexual encounters with others. This dynamic is frequently associated with consensual humiliation (for the "cuck"), compersion, and a specific form of power exchange. "Cuck" is a common slang term.

No-B.S. Context: This is an advanced kink dynamic, not just a label for a partner who is "okay" with non-monogamy. While some practitioners focus on consensual humiliation, others engage in the dynamic purely for the intense feeling of compersion it can evoke. When done ethically, it requires immense trust, security, and meticulous negotiation. When done unethically, it can be a mask for emotional abuse or coercion.

See Also: BDSM, Compersion, Hotwife, Kink.

D

DADT (Don't Ask, Don't Tell)

An open relationship model that permits outside sexual experiences, but they are never to be discussed.

No-B.S. Context: This is mutually agreed-upon lying. It makes informed consent about sexual health impossible.

See Also: Open Relationship.

De-escalation

A compassionate, intentional shift to reduce a relationship's intensity or commitment to a more sustainable level.

No-B.S. Context: This is a shape change, not a failure.

See Also: Relationship Escalator.

Demisexual

Describes individuals who only experience sexual attraction after forming a strong emotional bond.

No-B.S. Context: For a demisexual person, the emotional connection is the foundation from which sexual desire can grow. It challenges the common assumption that attraction is instantaneous.

See Also: Asexual (Ace), Aromantic (Aro).

Descriptive Hierarchy

A way of acknowledging existing life entanglements (like marriage or shared children) without imposing rules on other relationships.

No-B.S. Context: This is the ethical way to talk about hierarchy. It's an honest statement of capacity ("I can't offer cohabitation"), not a rule to control ("you can't fall in love").

See Also: Hierarchy, Prescriptive Hierarchy.

D/s (Dominance/Submission)

A consensual dynamic involving the exchange of power and authority between partners. It is one of the core components of BDSM. The person taking on the power role is the Dominant (Dom), and the person consensually giving power is the submissive (sub).

No-B.S. Context: These are roles, not personality types. The power in a D/s dynamic is a temporary gift that is intentionally granted, not taken, and it exists only within pre-negotiated boundaries. An ethical Dominant is obsessed with their submissive's well-being and consent. A person who uses the "Dom" label to justify being an unaccountable asshole is not a Dom; they are an abuser.

See Also: BDSM, Power Exchange, Protocol.

Dyad

A group of two people; a pair. In the context of relationships, it refers to a couple or a two-person partnership.

No-B.S. Context: While it simply means a pair, this term is useful in ENM for neutrally describing a two-person relationship without the cultural baggage of the word "couple."

See Also: Couple Privilege, Hierarchy.

E

Emotional Hot Potato

An unethical trap where a partner refuses to acknowledge the impact of their actions, instead treating their partner's resulting feelings as a problem for them to solve alone.

No-B.S. Context: This often comes disguised in therapy-speak like, "That's your trigger to work on." While we are all responsible for our reactions, this tactic is used to evade accountability for the action that caused the reaction. It is a denial of co-regulation.

See Also: Co-regulation, Weaponized Therapy-Speak.

Enablers

In the context of community dynamics, individuals who protect a harmful person from accountability, often to maintain social peace or their own status.

No-B.S. Context: Enablers are the structural support for toxic behavior in a community. Their silence or active defense allows harm to continue. Recognizing enablers is as important as identifying the primary source of harm.

See Also: Missing Stair, Abuse, Red Flag.

ENM (Ethical Non-Monogamy)

An umbrella term for relationship models where partners have multiple intimate connections with the full, informed consent of everyone involved.

No-B.S Context: The key word here is ethical.

See Also: Polyamory, Swinging, Open Relationship.

Envy

Wanting something someone else has.

No-B.S. Context: Unlike jealousy (which fears loss), envy focuses on what you lack. It's about desire, not threat.

See Also: Jealousy.

Exhibitionist

A person who derives pleasure from being watched by others, particularly during sexual activity.

No-B.S. Context: This is an active form of participation, not a passive one. Ethical voyeurism requires respecting the privacy of a scene and ensuring that those being watched have consented to an audience.

See Also: Kink, Scene, Voyeur.

F

Fluid Bonding

An agreement between partners to stop using barriers (e.g., condoms) for activities with STI risks.

No-B.S. Context: This is a high-trust, high-risk decision requiring a strict protocol. Breaching this agreement is a profound betrayal.

See Also: Safer Sex.

Full Swap

A term from the swinging community that describes partners engaging in a wide range of sexual activities with others, including penetrative sex.

No-B.S. Context: Often seen as the alternative to a "soft swap." Clear communication is essential, as one couple's definition of "full" may differ from another's.

See Also: Soft Swap, Swinging.

G

Garden Walkthrough

A light, capacity-aware relationship walkthrough. Partners notice willingness, size the pass to the lower-capacity partner, look together without trying to fix everything, choose only what both agree to touch now, and translate that into small, dated, visible actions with a brief follow-up and a forward-looking plan.

Gaslighting

An insidious form of emotional abuse where a person manipulates someone into doubting their own perceptions, memory, or sanity.

No-B.S. Context: This is a tactic of control designed to make you think you're the "crazy" one.

See Also: Abuse, Red Flag, Weaponized Therapy-Speak.

Green Flag

A behavior or dynamic that signals a high degree of emotional maturity, self-awareness, and ethical integrity.

No-B.S. Context: Green flags are not just the absence of red flags; they are positive indicators of a healthy capacity for repair. Examples include speaking about exes with respect, welcoming conversations about boundaries, and taking accountability without defensiveness.

See Also: Red Flag, Yellow Flag.

H

Hierarchy

A relationship structure where partners are assigned different levels of priority or power.

No-B.S. Context: Can be Descriptive (ethical) or Prescriptive (unethical). The difference is between acknowledging reality and controlling others.

See Also: Couple Privilege, Descriptive Hierarchy, Prescriptive Hierarchy, Veto.

Hinge

The individual in a polyamorous relationship who is dating two different people who are not dating each other. This person acts as the central connection point between the other two partners.

No-B.S. Context: Being a good hinge is one of the most demanding roles in polyamory. It requires impeccable communication, strong emotional boundaries, and a refusal to create drama between partners.

See Also: Metamour, Polycule, Squeaky Hinge, Triangulation, Vee.

Hotwife

A dynamic, typically in swinging, where a married or committed woman has sexual relationships with other partners with the full knowledge and often encouragement of her primary partner.

No-B.S. Context: This dynamic can be empowering when centered on the woman's agency and desire. It becomes unethical when it serves as a performative role to fulfill a partner's fantasy without her full, enthusiastic consent.

See Also: Bull, Cuckold / Cuckquean, Swinging, One Penis Policy (OPP).

I

Intimacy

The experience of deep connection, closeness, and vulnerability with another person.

No-B.S. Context: Our culture often assumes intimacy is synonymous with sex. A core practice of ENM is to decouple these concepts.

See Also: Access Intimacy, Platonic Partnership, Sex.

J

Jealousy

A complex emotional response to a perceived threat to a valued relationship.

No-B.S. Context: Jealousy is not a moral failing but a signal—a smoke alarm—of unmet needs or insecurities.

See Also: Compersion, Envy, Smoke Alarm.

K

Kink

A broad term for non-conventional sexualities, desires, and practices.

No-B.S. Context: Ethical kink requires meticulous negotiation and consent; misusing kink dynamics to justify control is abuse.

See Also: BDSM.

KTP (Kitchen Table Polyamory)

A style of polyamory where the ideal is that all members of a relationship network are comfortable interacting together casually, as if they could all share coffee at the kitchen table.

No-B.S. Context: KTP is beautiful when it arises organically but becomes toxic and coercive when it is a requirement.

See Also: Metamour, Parallel Polyamory.

L

Lifestyle, The (LS)

A common slang term, particularly within the swinging community, to refer to the subculture of consensual non-monogamy.

No-B.S. Context: While predominantly a swinger term, it is sometimes used more broadly by older ENM practitioners as a general term for the subculture. In this guide, we use it to refer to the social scene, not the identity itself.

See Also: ENM, Swinging.

Love Bombing

A manipulative tactic where a person floods a new partner with excessive, premature affection to create a fast, intense attachment.

No-B.S. Context: The red flag is not the affection itself but the intention: to bypass boundaries and make the recipient dependent.

See Also: Abuse, Red Flag, Trauma Bond.

M

Metamour

Your partner's other partner, with whom you share no romantic or sexual relationship.

No-B.S. Context: Navigating this relationship is a unique and foundational challenge in polyamory.

See Also: Hinge, KTP, Parallel Polyamory.

Missing Stair

A term for a harmful person within a social group whom the group enables by warning newcomers to "avoid that stair" instead of removing the person.

No-B.S. Context: A sign of a dysfunctional and unsafe community.

See Also: Abuse, Enablers, Red Flag.

Monogamish

A mostly monogamous relationship with specific, agreed-upon exceptions for outside sexual activity.

No-B.S. Context: The term was coined by Dan Savage.

See Also: Open Relationship.

Monogamy Mindset

The collection of unexamined, culturally inherited scripts and assumptions about how love "should" work. Its core tenets often include the ideas that love is scarce, exclusivity equals value, and every relationship must follow the Relationship Escalator.

No-B.S. Context: You can practice ENM while still being controlled by these unconscious assumptions—and it will sabotage your relationships. The work is to make these scripts conscious so you can choose which ones to keep.

See Also: Amatonormativity, Inherited Script, Mononormativity, Relationship Escalator.

Mononormativity

The unexamined, society-wide assumption that having only one romantic and sexual partner at a time (monogamy) is the only normal, healthy, or moral way to build a life.

No-B.S. Context: This is the script that asks, "But who's your *real* partner?" It's the source of the belief that jealousy is proof of love and that loving more than one person means you love your primary partner less. It directly stigmatizes polyamory and open relationships.

See Also: Amatonormativity, Monogamy Mindset.

N

Nesting Partner

A partner with whom you live and share a domestic life.

No-B.S. Context: This logistical entanglement often creates a de facto hierarchy. Transparency about this dynamic is key.

See Also: Anchor Partner, Hierarchy.

NRE (New Relationship Energy)

The intense excitement and often reality-distorting euphoria felt at the start of a new relationship.

No-B.S. Context: NRE is a thrilling but temporary form of insanity that can blind you to red flags and lead to neglecting existing partners.

See Also: Compersion, Jealousy, ORE (Old Relationship Energy).

O

One Penis Policy (OPP)

A rule in swinging where a man allows his female partner to play sexually only with other women, not other men.

No-B.S. Context: This is often rooted in hetero-patriarchal control and biphobia.

See Also: Biphobia, Swinging.

Open Relationship

A broad term for a relationship where partners agree to some form of sexual and/or romantic connection with others.

No-B.S. Context: The term is dangerously vague without specific, negotiated agreements.

See Also: DADT, Monogamish, Swinging.

ORE (Old Relationship Energy) / ERE (Established Relationship Energy)

The comfortable, deep, and secure energy of a long-term relationship.

No-B.S. Context: ORE is the quiet, life-sustaining sun to NRE's brilliant, hot bonfire.

See Also: NRE (New Relationship Energy).

P

Parallel Polyamory

A style of polyamory where metamours have minimal or no direct contact, with their shared partner acting as the communication bridge.

No-B.S. Context: A valid and healthy choice for those who value privacy.

See Also: Kitchen Table Polyamory, Metamour.

Platonic Partnership

A committed relationship built on deep platonic love rather than romantic or sexual attraction.

No-B.S. Context: These relationships challenge amatonormativity by centering platonic love as a valid foundation for a life partnership.

See Also: Chosen Family, Queerplatonic Partnership (QPP).

Polyamory

The practice of having multiple consensual romantic and emotionally intimate relationships simultaneously.

No-B.S. Context: It is defined by the acceptance of ongoing emotional intimacy, which distinguishes it from swinging.

See Also: ENM.

Polycule

The entire network of people linked through non-monogamous relationships.

No-B.S. Context: A simple way to think of it is as a "relationship molecule."

See Also: Hinge, Metamour, Triad, Vee.

Polysaturation

The point at which your capacity is fully reached, and adding more partners would harm your well-being or existing relationships.

No-B.S. Context: Recognizing polysaturation is a critical ethical skill. Saying "no" is more ethical than overcommitting and neglecting everyone.

See Also: Burnout, Capacity.

Polyswinger

A person or couple who practices a hybrid of polyamory and swinging. They typically maintain long-term, emotionally intimate relationships (polyamory) while also participating in casual, recreational group sex (swinging).

No-B.S. Context: This term acknowledges that the line between relationship styles can be blurry. The key ethical challenge is maintaining crystal-clear communication about the nature and intention of each individual connection.

See Also: Polyamory, Swinging.

Power Exchange

A consensual dynamic where one partner gives up control to another within negotiated boundaries.

No-B.S. Context: A core element of BDSM. The power is a gift that is intentionally and temporarily granted, not taken.

See Also: BDSM, D/s.

Prescriptive Hierarchy

A relationship structure that uses rules to enforce a power imbalance between partners, typically to protect a "primary" relationship.

No-B.S. Context: This is where hierarchy becomes unethical. It's the source of controlling rules like the veto.

See Also: Couple Privilege, Descriptive Hierarchy, Hierarchy, Veto.

Primary Partner

In a hierarchical relationship structure, the partner who is given the most priority in terms of time, life decisions, or emotional investment.

No-B.S. Context: This is a formal rank, distinct from an "anchor partner," which describes a feeling of stability rather than a structural priority.

See Also: Anchor Partner, Hierarchy.

Protocol

In BDSM, pre-agreed rules, rituals, or behaviors that structure a power dynamic.

No-B.S. Context: Ethical protocols are co-created to enhance the experience and ensure safety, not to exert control outside of the agreed-upon dynamic.

See Also: D/s, Scene.

Q

Queer

A broad and often reclaimed umbrella term for identities, sexualities, and relationship styles that diverge from normative cisgender, heterosexual, and monogamous expectations.

No-B.S. Context: "Queer" can be both an **identity** (a word for a person or community) and a **political action** (the verb "to queer," meaning to challenge, question, or deconstruct a norm). This book uses it in both senses, recognizing that choosing to live and love outside the inherited scripts is, in itself, a queer act.

See Also: Gender Identity, Sexual Orientation.

Queerplatonic Partnership (QPP)

A committed, emotionally intense relationship that may not involve romantic or sexual attraction.

No-B.S. Context: This term was coined to give language to a platonic bond that feels as significant as a romantic one.

See Also: Aromantic (Aro), Platonic Partnership.

R

Red Flag

A warning sign of potentially harmful behavior, intentions, or dynamics.

No-B.S. Context: In ENM, this includes behaviors like love bombing, ignoring boundaries, or weaponized therapy-speak.

See Also: Abuse, Gaslighting, Love Bombing, Missing Stair, Yellow Flag.

Relationship Anarchy (RA)

A radical philosophy that rejects all societal norms around relationships, rejecting hierarchies and building each connection from the ground up based on individual desires and agreements.

No-B.S. Context: RA is not an excuse to be a flake; it demands radical accountability.

See Also: Autonomy, Hierarchy, Solo Polyamory.

Relationship Escalator

The default, inherited script of societal expectations for how relationships "should" progress: dating, exclusivity, cohabitation, marriage, and children.

No-B.S. Context: ENM, in all its forms, often involves consciously stepping off this prescribed path.

See Also: Amatonormativity, De-escalation.

Repair

The ongoing effort to heal a relationship and rebuild trust after a rupture.

No-B.S. Context: It demands full accountability and mutual willingness to engage.

See Also: Accountability, "Good Enough" Relationship, Rupture.

Rule

A directive about what another person can or cannot do, often stemming from one's own fear or inexperience.

No-B.S. Context: Rules ("You can't…") differ from boundaries (self-focused) and agreements (collaborative). They can serve as healthy "training wheels" but become toxic "cages" when permanent and controlling.

See Also: Agreement, Boundary, Trellis.

Rupture

A significant breach in connection or trust caused by conflict or broken agreements.

No-B.S. Context: Ruptures are inevitable but can foster growth when addressed with care and repair.

See Also: Accountability, Repair.

S

Safer Sex

Practices to minimize the risk of sexually transmitted infections (STIs), such as using barriers, regular testing, and open communication.

No-B.S. Context: This recognizes that no sexual activity other than abstinence is 100% "safe."

See Also: Fluid Bonding, Sex.

Safeword

A pre-agreed word or signal used to instantly stop or pause a BDSM scene.

No-B.S. Context: Safewords are sacred; ignoring them is a severe consent violation.

See Also: BDSM, Consent, Scene, Traffic Light System.

Scene

In BDSM, a pre-negotiated period of play with clearly defined roles, activities, and safety protocols.

No-B.S. Context: A scene is a container, not a relationship. Consent is specific and time-bound: what's negotiated is in; everything else is out. Roles apply only inside the scene unless you both extend them. Either person can stop at any time—no justification needed.

See Also: Aftercare, BDSM, Protocol, Safeword.

Sex

A term with no single, universally agreed-upon definition, which can include a wide range of physical acts intended for pleasure or connection.

No-B.S. Context: The most dangerous inherited script is the assumption that you and your partners mean the same thing when you use this word. A massive number of betrayals happen because agreements were built on a vague, unexamined definition. Define your terms.

See Also: Agreement, Safer Sex.

Sexual Orientation

A person's pattern of emotional, romantic, and/or sexual attraction to other people.

No-B.S. Context: Your sexual orientation is your own to define; it does not obligate you to be attracted to everyone who fits a certain category. Do not let anyone weaponize your identity against you.

See Also: Biphobia, Queer.

Solo Polyamory (SoPo)

A polyamorous approach prioritizing autonomy, where an individual considers themselves their own primary partner.

No-B.S. Context: This is a relationship philosophy focused on building an autonomous life with multiple committed relationships. This focus on intentional relationship-building distinguishes it from a dating style centered on casual sexual connections.

See Also: Anchor Partner, Autonomy, Relationship Anarchy.

Soft Swap

A term from the swinging community where partners agree to engage in sexual activities with others that intentionally exclude certain acts, most commonly penetrative sex.

No-B.S. Context: This is a common and responsible way for couples to begin exploring swinging, as it allows them to expand their boundaries gradually and within a clearly defined container.

See Also: Full Swap, Swinging.

Spoons / Spoon Theory

A metaphor for the limited energy available for daily tasks, particularly for those with chronic illnesses or disabilities.

No-B.S. Context: Each task consumes "spoons," which may not replenish quickly. Understanding this is key to supporting partners with limited capacity.

See Also: Access Intimacy, Capacity.

Squeaky Hinge

A problematic dynamic where the hinge in a relationship causes friction between their partners through poor communication or boundary management.

No-B.S. Context: This is a common failure mode, often involving triangulation or emotional dumping. The hinge, overwhelmed and conflict-avoidant, makes their stress everyone else's problem instead of taking responsibility for their central role.

See Also: Hinge, Triangulation.

Swinging

A form of ENM centered on sexual encounters with others, typically practiced by a committed couple.

No-B.S. Context: It differs from polyamory by prioritizing recreational sex over the formation of ongoing emotional bonds.

See Also: One Penis Policy (OPP), Open Relationship, The Lifestyle (LS).

T

Threatening Presence

A form of physical intimidation and coercive control where a person uses their body or proximity to instill fear and manipulate a partner's behavior without overt violence.

No-B.S. Context: This isn't just "making someone uncomfortable." It's a specific abuse tactic.

See Also: Abuse, Coercion, Red Flag.

Traffic Light System

A common, non-verbal safeword system used in kink and play spaces.

No-B.S. Context: * Green Light: A verbal check-in ("Green light") meaning "I am good, everything is great, continue or escalate." * **Yellow Light:** A verbal safeword ("Yellow light") meaning "Slow down, check in, something is becoming too intense or needs adjustment." * **Red Light:** A verbal safeword ("Red light") meaning "Stop immediately, end the scene now, no questions asked." This is a hard stop.

See Also: Safeword, Scene.

Trauma Bond

A strong, dysfunctional attachment between an abuser and the person they are abusing, created through a repeating cycle of abuse followed by intermittent kindness.

No-B.S. Context: This is not a healthy bond. It's an addictive attachment rooted in survival instincts.

See Also: Abuse, Gaslighting, Love Bombing.

Trellis

A key component of the Garden Metaphor, representing a temporary, supportive rule designed to help a new or vulnerable part of a relationship grow.

No-B.S. Context: A healthy rule is a trellis; it has a built-in plan for its own review and potential removal. An unhealthy rule is a cage; it is permanent and designed only to control, ultimately choking the connection it was meant to support.

See Also: Agreement, Boundary, Garden Metaphor, Rule.

Triad

A three-person relationship where each member is romantically involved with the others, also known as a "throuple."

No-B.S. Context: While often romanticized, the stable triad is a rare and complex dynamic. It requires managing the needs of three individuals and four distinct relationships simultaneously.

See Also: Polycule, Vee.

Triangulation

A harmful communication pattern where one person avoids direct conflict with another by involving a third party.

No-B.S. Context: In ENM, it's a frequent hinge failure that damages multiple relationships.

See Also: Hinge, Squeaky Hinge.

U

Unicorn

A slang term for a solo person (often a bisexual woman) willing to date or engage with a pre-existing couple.

No-B.S. Context: While the term is often used pejoratively to imply an objectified fantasy figure, many solo individuals actively and happily seek out these dynamics. The ethical focus is on ensuring the "unicorn" is treated as a whole person and equal participant, not an accessory.

See Also: Couple Privilege, Unicorn Hunting.

Unicorn Hunting

The unethical practice where a couple seeks a third partner (a "unicorn") to join their relationship as an accessory, without regard for that person's autonomy, desires, or emotional needs.

No-B.S. Context: This is defined by its objectification and toxic couple privilege. Key signs include having a list of pre-written rules, expecting the third to have no needs of their own, and treating the person as disposable. This is not ethical ENM; it is consumption.

See Also: Couple Privilege, Red Flag, Unicorn.

V

Vanilla

A slang term for anything considered conventional, mainstream, or not part of the ENM/kink subcultures.

No-B.S. Context: This is a flexible term of contrast. It most often describes non-kinky sex ("vanilla sex"), but can also refer to monogamous relationships ("a vanilla relationship"), people who are not in the lifestyle ("my vanilla friends"), or a non-play social event where everyone keeps their clothes on ("it's a vanilla party").

See Also: BDSM, Kink.

Vee

A polyamorous configuration where one person (the hinge) is romantically or sexually involved with two others who are not involved with each other.

No-B.S. Context: The most prevalent polyamorous structure.

See Also: Hinge, Triad, Polycule.

Veto

A rule in hierarchical ENM allowing one partner to demand the end of another's separate relationship.

No-B.S. Context: Often unethical, as it undermines autonomy and treats "secondary" partners as disposable.

See Also: Autonomy, Hierarchy, Rule.

Voyeur

A person who derives pleasure from watching others engage in sexual or intimate activity.

No-B.S. Context: This is an active form of participation, not a passive one. Ethical voyeurism requires respecting the privacy of a scene and ensuring that those being watched have consented to an audience.

See Also: Exhibitionist, Scene.

W

Weaponized Therapy-Speak

Using psychological jargon to manipulate, dismiss, or control.

No-B.S. Context: Examples include saying, "You're just projecting" or "That's your trauma response," to dodge accountability.

See Also: Abuse, Emotional Hot Potato, Gaslighting, Red Flag.

Yellow Flag

A behavior or dynamic that gives pause and calls for a curious conversation. Unlike a red flag, it is not necessarily a sign of danger, but rather an indicator of potential incompatibility, inexperience, or a blind spot that needs to be addressed.

No-B.S. Context: The goal is not to pathologize every mistake. A yellow flag is a prompt to slow down and ask more questions. A partner's willingness to discuss a yellow flag is often a green flag.

See Also: Green Flag, Red Flag.

REFERENCES

This book is a compass, not the entire map. The journey of building ethical, authentic relationships is a lifelong practice of learning and unlearning. The following list is not a required reading assignment; it is an armory of tools and a library of wisdom from the thinkers, researchers, and rebels who have shaped this landscape.

A "no-bullshit" approach requires engaging with these texts critically. Many are foundational, but some are also flawed, dated, or simplify complex realities into marketable *"pop psychology."* This guide will help you take the wisdom, identify the problems, and use these works to forge your own path.

THE 'HOW-TO' GUIDES: STARTING YOUR JOURNEY

Hardy, Janet W., *and Dossie Easton. 2017. The Ethical Slut: A Practical Guide to Polyamory, Open Relationships, and Other Freedoms in Sex and Love. 3rd ed. Berkeley, CA: Ten Speed Press.*

> **Analysis:** *The original, revolutionary text that gave a generation a language for ENM. Its great strength is its joyous, shame-free sex-positivity. However, it should be read with a critical eye. Its boundless optimism can feel disconnected from the intense emotional labor that real-world ENM requires, and its "free love" ethos can inadvertently create a pressure to perform a kind of effortless, "enlightened" happiness that this book directly*

critiques. The 3rd edition is a necessary update that addresses some of the couple-centric bias of its earlier versions.

Taormino, Tristan. 2008. *Opening Up: A Guide to Creating and Sustaining Open Relationships.* San Francisco, CA: Cleis Press.

> **Analysis:** *An intensely practical, if dated, textbook on the logistics of opening up. Its strength is its structured, step-by-step approach. Its significant problem is its deep-seated couple-centrism, which provides a blueprint for the exact kind of prescriptive, unethical hierarchy this book warns against. It is a useful guide to the mechanics of a particular model, but it is not a guide to the modern ethics of prioritizing the autonomy of all individuals involved.*

Anapol, Deborah. 2010. *Polyamory in the 21st Century: Love and Intimacy with Multiple Partners.* Lanham, MD: Rowman & Littlefield.

> **Analysis:** *One of the pioneering texts on polyamory from a clinical psychologist. Anapol's work brings a more holistic, spiritual, and psychological lens to the practice, exploring concepts like compersion and sacred sexuality. Its primary value is in providing historical context from one of the field's early experts, though the spiritual framing may not resonate with all readers.*

THE CORE TOOLKIT: MANAGING EMOTIONS & COMMUNICATION

Fern, Jessica. 2020. *Polysecure: Attachment, Trauma, and Consensual Non-monogamy.* Portland, OR: Thorntree Press.

> **Analysis:** *The definitive modern text on the emotional architecture of ENM. This book is the clinical, trauma-informed antidote to the prescriptive simplifications of pop psychology. Fern brilliantly translates complex attachment theory into a practical framework (the S.E.C.U.R.E. model) for building security in non-traditional relationship structures. It is arguably the most important and practical guide to the internal work of ENM available today.*

Rosenberg, Marshall B. *2015. Nonviolent Communication: A Language of Life.* 3rd ed. Encinitas, CA: PuddleDancer Press.

> **Analysis:** *The source of the brilliant four-step framework this book adapts. The NVC model is a powerful tool. However, the book itself can be deeply problematic. Its tone is often sanctimonious, and the stilted, therapeutic language it advocates for can feel inauthentic and is easily weaponized to shut down conversations or feign vulnerability. This book should be treated as a technical manual for a powerful engine, not as a script for how to be a human.*

Aguilar, Joreth. *2018. Jealousy: A Guide to Managing it in Polyamorous and Open Relationships.* Thornapple Publishing.

> **Analysis:** *A refreshingly practical and non-dogmatic workbook. It successfully avoids pop psychology platitudes by treating jealousy not as a personal failing to be overcome, but as a functional signal—a "smoke alarm"—that needs to be investigated with curiosity. Its hands-on approach is an excellent resource.*

Lerner, Harriet. *2017. Why Won't You Apologize?: Healing Big Betrayals and Everyday Hurts.* New York, NY: Touchstone.

> **Analysis:** *A masterclass in accountability from a clinical psychologist. Lerner's work is the antidote to the non-apologies and blame-shifting that are common in relational conflict. It provides a sharp, clear-eyed analysis of what constitutes a real repair, making it an essential tool.*

Brown, Brené. *2015. Rising Strong: The Reckoning. The Rumble. The Revolution.* New York, NY: Spiegel & Grau.

> **Analysis:** *Provides a research-backed, three-stage framework for learning from failure and navigating emotional difficulty. Offers a practical, shame-resilient process for the hard work of repair and getting back up after a relational rupture. It is not ENM-specific; the core concepts must be adapted by the reader.*

Gottman, John M. *, and Nan Silver. 2015. The Seven Principles for Making Marriage Work.* New York, NY: Harmony Books.

Analysis: *A foundational work based on decades of quantitative research. Its diagnostic tools (like the "Four Horsemen") are invaluable. However, it is a form of "pop science" in its application, presenting a formulaic approach to relationships that is exclusively focused on the monogamous married couple. Its insights into dyadic communication are useful, but its one-size-fits-all model runs contrary to the co-created, bespoke nature of ENM agreements.*

Levine, Amir, and Rachel S. *F. Heller. 2010. Attached: The New Science of Adult Attachment and How It Can Help You Find—and Keep—Love. New York, NY: TarcherPerigee.*

Analysis: *The quintessential pop psychology translation of attachment theory. Its strength is making the basic concepts (secure, anxious, avoidant) accessible. Its significant problem is its prescriptive, often pathologizing, and deeply mononormative framework, which is geared toward finding "The One." It can be a useful starting point for identifying your patterns, but Polysecure is the essential and far superior text for applying these concepts to ENM.*

THE ETHICAL BOTTOM LINE: SAFETY, ABUSE, & COERCIVE CONTROL

Bancroft, Lundy. *2002. Why Does He Do That?: Inside the Minds of Angry and Controlling Men. New York, NY: Berkley Books.*

Analysis: *A life-saving, foundational text. This is the antithesis of pop psychology. It is a brutally clear, practical, and reality-based guide to the mindset of abusers. Its central thesis—that abuse is a problem of entitlement and control, not pathology or trauma—is a non-negotiable starting point for anyone seeking to understand interpersonal violence. Its explicit gender focus is a limitation, but the patterns it describes are universally applicable.*

Stark, Evan. *2007. Coercive Control: How Men Entrap Women in Personal Life. New York, NY: Oxford University Press.*

Analysis: *The key academic text that provides the legal and sociological framework for understanding abuse not as a series of violent incidents, but* as an ongoing strategy of control. This is the scholarly backbone for the arguments made in Bancroft's work and in this book's chapter on abuse.

van der Kolk, Bessel A. 2014. *The Body Keeps the Score: Brain, Mind, and Body in the Healing of Trauma.* New York, NY: Viking.

Analysis: The definitive clinical work on how trauma is stored in the body. It provides the hard science behind the "no-bullshit" advice to trust your gut feelings and somatic responses over the gaslighting of a manipulator. It is dense and can be triggering, but it is an essential resource for understanding the physiological reality of safety and threat.

Hassan, Steven. 2013. *Freedom of Mind: Helping Loved Ones Leave Controlling People, Cults, and Beliefs.* Newton, MA: Freedom of Mind Press.

Analysis: Provides the BITE model (Behavior, Information, Thought, Emotion), a clear and practical diagnostic tool for identifying the structures of coercive control in groups. It is an essential, reality-based checklist.

Lalich, Janja, and Madeleine Tobias. 2006. *Take Back Your Life: Recovering from Cults and Abusive Relationships.* Berkeley, CA: Bay Tree Publishing.

Analysis: A practical guide for survivors of cults and high-control relationships, focusing on the recovery process. An excellent resource for the "what's next" after leaving a toxic dynamic.

THE BIG PICTURE: SOCIAL, POLITICAL, & HISTORICAL CONTEXT

Hooks, Bell. 2000. *All About Love: New Visions.* New York, NY: William Morrow.

Analysis: A profound work of philosophy that serves as a powerful antidote to the superficiality of pop psychology. hooks redefines love as an ethical verb—a practice of care and commitment—providing a deep moral and political grounding for the work of building authentic relationships.

Gahran, Amy. 2017. *Stepping Off the Relationship Escalator: Uncommon Love and Life.* Off the Escalator Enterprises.

Analysis: The definitive guide to the concept of the "Relationship Escalator." It gives a crucial name and framework to the default societal script that this book seeks to dismantle. Essential reading for anyone practicing a non-escalator style of relating.

Brake, Elizabeth. 2012. Minimizing Marriage: Marriage, Morality, and the Law. New York, NY: Oxford University Press.

Analysis: The academic backbone for the critique of amatonormativity. This rigorous philosophical work provides the intellectual grounding for valuing platonic and other non-traditional partnerships. It is a dense, academic text, not a casual read.

Illouz, Eva. 2019. The End of Love: A Sociology of Negative Relations. New York, NY: Oxford University Press.

Analysis: A powerful sociological critique of modern romance. Illouz argues that capitalism and rational choice have created a culture of "un-loving" (ghosting, casual disposability). Her work provides the essential, sobering context for the frustrations of modern dating, showing that these are systemic problems, not personal failings.

Hochschild, Arlie Russell. (1983) 2012. The Managed Heart: Commercialization of Human Feeling. Updated ed. Berkeley, CA: University of California Press.

Analysis: The landmark sociological study that coined the term "emotional labor." It provides the essential framework for understanding the often invisible, unpaid emotional work required to sustain relationships, a concept central to this book's analysis of burnout and capacity.

Gilligan, Carol. 1982. In a Different Voice: Psychological Theory and Women's Development. Cambridge, MA: Harvard University Press.

Analysis: The landmark work of feminist psychology that launched the "Ethics of Care." Gilligan challenged traditional models of moral development and instead centered a morality based on relationships, interdependence, and responsibility to others, providing the foundational philosophical argument for a "Care Web."

hooks, bell. 2004. *The Will to Change: Men, Masculinity, and Love.* New York, NY: Atria Books.

>   **Analysis:** *A profound and compassionate critique of patriarchal masculinity. hooks argues that men have been socialized to betray their emotional selves to conform to patriarchal ideals, preventing them from truly giving and receiving love. A must-read for understanding the internal landscape of men and a perfect companion piece to Chapter 28.*

Barker, Meg-John. 2018. *Rewriting the Rules: An Anti-Self-Help Guide to Love, Sex and Relationships.* 2nd ed. London: Routledge.

>   **Analysis:** *A broad, queer-inclusive, and accessible guide to the philosophy of questioning norms and consciously designing your own ways of living and loving.*

Perel, Esther. 2017. *The State of Affairs: Rethinking Infidelity.* New York, NY: Harper.

>   **Analysis:** *A nuanced look at infidelity, exploring the complex meanings and motivations behind affairs. Provides a compassionate framework for understanding betrayal, which is useful for couples opening up after infidelity, but is not a guide to ENM.*

Ryan, Christopher, and Cacilda Jethá. 2010. *Sex at Dawn: The Prehistoric Origins of Modern Sexuality.* New York, NY: Harper Perennial.

>   **Analysis:** *A massively influential book that functions as a powerful cultural "thought experiment" against the idea of innate monogamy. It should be read critically; its scientific claims have been heavily contested by many professional anthropologists, and it is best understood as a provocative pop science narrative rather than settled academic fact.*

Engels, Friedrich. (1884) 2010. *The Origin of the Family, Private Property and the State.* London: Penguin Classics.

>   **Analysis:** *The classic Marxist argument that the monogamous nuclear family is an economic structure tied to the emergence of private property and the need to control inheritance. A historical document, not a reflection of modern scholarship.*

Weston, Kath. *1991. Families We Choose: Lesbians, Gays, Kinship. New York, NY: Columbia University Press.*

> **Analysis:** *The classic anthropological work that introduced and documented the concept of "chosen family" in LGBTQ+ communities as a crucial survival strategy against societal and familial rejection.*

Franke, Katherine. *2016. Wedlocked: The Perils of Marriage Equality. New York, NY: NYU Press.*

> **Analysis:** *A powerful legal critique arguing that the fight for marriage equality has, paradoxically, reinforced the power of the state to define and regulate relationships, further marginalizing all non-marital family forms. Provides the essential legal context for understanding why creating private contracts is a necessary political act.*

Combahee River Collective. *(1977) 2017. A Black Feminist Statement. In Toward a Black Feminist Criticism, by Barbara Smith. Brooklyn, NY: The CUNY Feminist Press.*

> **Analysis:** *The foundational text of the Combahee River Collective, a Black lesbian feminist organization. This statement articulates the concept of "intersectionality"—the interlocking nature of systems of oppression. Its critique of patriarchal and racist structures and its vision of collective liberation provide a crucial political foundation for any truly radical reimagining of relationships and community.*

DEEP DIVES: SPECIFIC PRACTICES & COMMUNITIES

Nagoski, Emily. *2015. Come As You Are: The Surprising New Science That Will Transform Your Sex Life. New York, NY: Simon & Schuster.*

> **Analysis:** *A model of excellent science communication. Nagoski's work is an accessible, validating, and empowering guide to understanding sexual response that dismantles shame with scientific evidence.*

Wiseman, Jay. *2009. SM 101: A Realistic Introduction. 2nd ed. Emeryville, CA: Greenery Press.*

Analysis: *A comprehensive introductory guide to the practicalities and ethics of BDSM. It is a refreshingly grounded and realistic text relentlessly focused on safety and consent, making it the perfect "no-bullshit" entry point to kink.*

Bauer, R. *2014. "Queer BDSM and Kink: Embodied Politics and Play." In A Companion to Feminist Philosophy, edited by Ann Garry, Serene J. Khader, and Alison Stone, 486-98. Oxford, UK: Wiley-Blackwell.*

Analysis: *A representative academic essay on the philosophy of kink, treating it not merely as a set of practices but as a form of embodied political and ethical play. This type of scholarship provides a theoretical framework for understanding how consent, power, and identity are negotiated in BDSM.*

Sheff, Elisabeth. *2014. The Polyamorists Next Door: Inside Multiple-Partner Relationships and Families. Lanham, MD: Rowman & Littlefield.*

Analysis: *One of the most important long-term sociological studies of polyamorous families, offering invaluable, data-driven insights that counter stereotypes and speculation. It is descriptive, not prescriptive.*

Sheff, Elisabeth, ed. *2015. Stories from the Polycule: Real Life in Polyamorous Families. Portland, OR: Thorntree Press.*

Analysis: *An edited collection of personal essays that provides invaluable qualitative insight into the day-to-day joys and challenges of polyamorous family life. A must-read for anyone who wants to understand the human experience behind the data.*

Mingus, Mia. *2011. Access Intimacy: The Missing Link. Leaving Evidence, May 5, 2011. https://leavingevidence.wordpress.com/2011/05/05/access-intimacy-the-missing-link/. Accessed August 5, 2025.*

Analysis: *A seminal essay required for understanding disability justice within relationships. Not academic theory, but a vital, lived-experience framework providing essential tools for compassionate partnership.*

REFERENCES

Miserandino, Christine. 2003. "The Spoon Theory." *But You Don't Look Sick.* *https://butyoudontlooksick.com/articles/written-by-christine/the-spoon-theory/.* Accessed August 5, 2025.

> **Analysis:** *A seminal essay required for understanding disability justice within relationships. Not academic theory, but a vital, lived-experience framework providing essential tools for compassionate partnership.*

Bogaert, Anthony F. 2012. *Understanding Asexuality.* Lanham, MD: Rowman & Littlefield.

> **Analysis:** *A foundational academic text by one of the world's leading researchers on human sexuality, providing a comprehensive overview of asexuality as a distinct sexual orientation. Essential for anyone seeking a scientific understanding of the 'A' in LGBTQIA+.*

Gould, Terry. 2000. *The Lifestyle: A Look at the Erotic Rites of Swingers.* Toronto, ON: Vintage Canada.

> **Analysis:** *An immersive journalistic and ethnographic exploration of the North American swinging community, providing invaluable context on the culture and social dynamics of 'The Lifestyle.'*

Nordgren, Andie. 2006. *The Short Instructional Manifesto for Relationship Anarchy. The Anarchist Library. https://theanarchistlibrary.org/library/andie-nordgren-the-short-instructional-manifesto-for-relationship-anarchy. Accessed August 5, 2025.*

> **Analysis:** *The foundational manifesto that coined the term and laid out the core principles of Relationship Anarchy. It is the essential, radical source text for the philosophy.*

Adams, Diana. n.d. *Diana Adams Law & Mediation.* Accessed August 5, 2025. *https://dianaadamslaw.net/*

> **Analysis:** *The website and resource hub for a leading lawyer specializing in legal protections for non-traditional families. A key resource for finding information on cohabitation agreements, parenting agreements, and estate planning.*

FURTHER ACADEMIC RESEARCH

Andersson, Charlotta. 2022. "Drawing the Line at Infidelity: Negotiating Relationship Agreements and Making Sense of Cheating in Consensual Non-Monogamy." Sexualities 25 (5–6): 629–46.

Analysis: An academic paper exploring how people in ENM relationships define "cheating" not as sex itself, but as the violation of explicitly negotiated agreements and trust.

Balzarini, Rhonda N., et al. 2019. "Perceptions of Primary and Secondary Relationships in Polyamory." PLoS ONE 14 (5): e0217267.

Analysis: An empirical study providing quantitative data that demonstrates the harm of prescriptive hierarchy on the well-being of "secondary" partners.

Conley, Terri D., et al. 2012. "The Fewer the Merrier?: Assessing Stigma Surrounding Consensually Non-Monogamous Romantic Relationships." Analyses of Social Issues and Public Policy 13 (1): 1–30.

Analysis: A key study that empirically demonstrates the social stigma faced by people in ENM relationships, but also finds that ENM relationships do not differ from monogamous ones on key measures of relationship quality.

Klesse, Christian. 2011. "The Dark Side of the Polyamorous Community." Sexualities 14 (6): 705–22.

Analysis: A seminal and unflinching academic critique of how polyamorous communities can replicate systems of power and exclusion, including issues of racism, sexism, and couple privilege.

Moors, Amy C., et al. 2015. "Attached to Monogamy? Avoidance, Anxiety, and People in Consensually Nonmonogamous Relationships." Journal of Social and Personal Relationships 32 (8): 981–1002.

Analysis: A study challenging the stereotype that people choose ENM because they are "commitment-phobic," suggesting that those high in attachment avoidance are actually more likely to prefer monogamy.

ABOUT THE AUTHORS

C.L. & D.J. Aaron are a writing team whose work is informed by their professional backgrounds in law, psychology, and education. After several years as practicing members of the ethical non-monogamy community, they saw a critical need for a guide that was both compassionate and brutally honest. The No-Bullshit Guide is the result: a practical toolkit for navigating modern relationships with integrity.

They write under a pen name to protect the privacy of their community, friends, and partners—an ethical practice at the heart of their work.

www.ingramcontent.com/pod-product-compliance
Lightning Source LLC
Chambersburg PA
CBHW032048020426
42335CB00011B/235